Y0-AKO-872

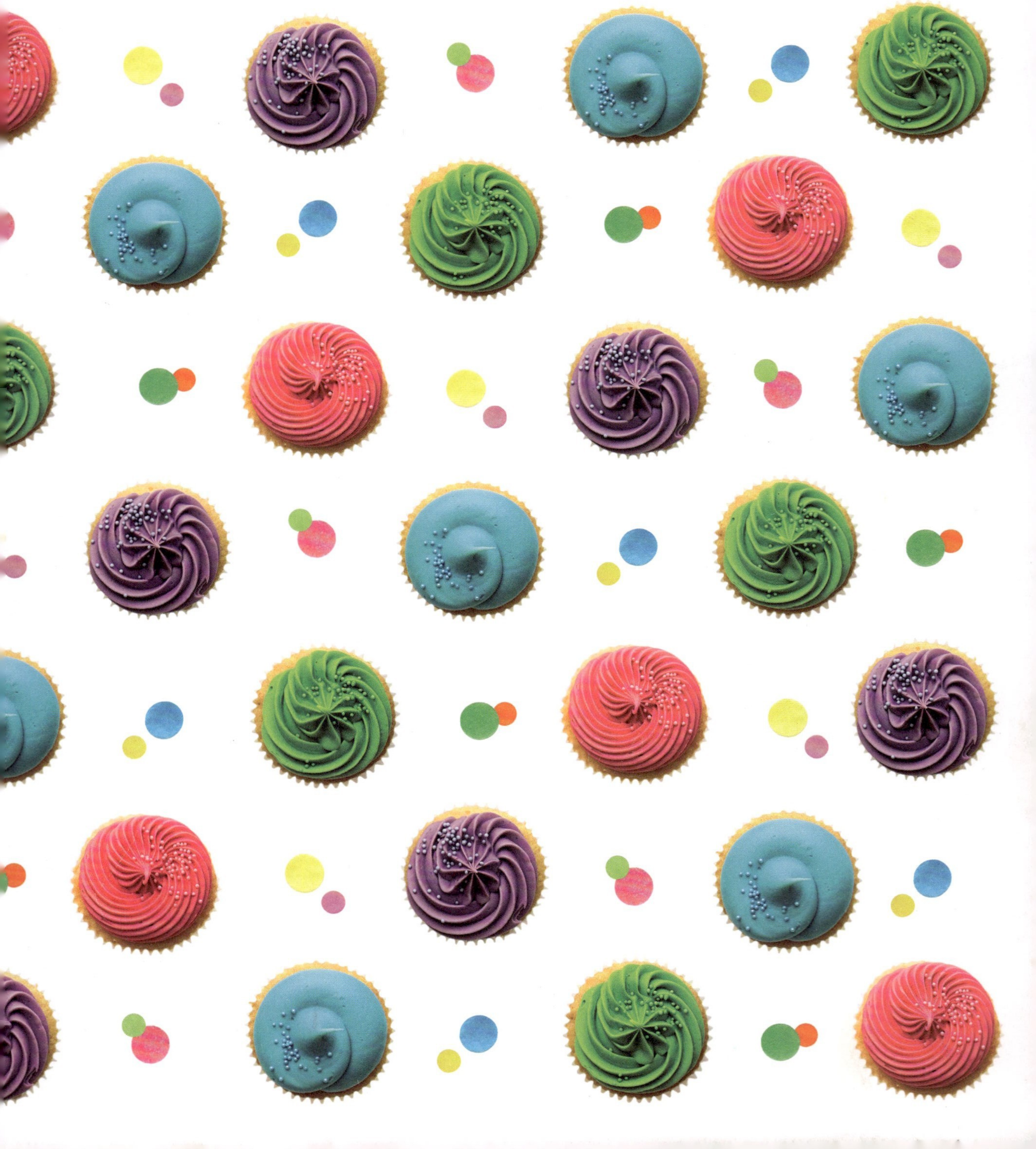

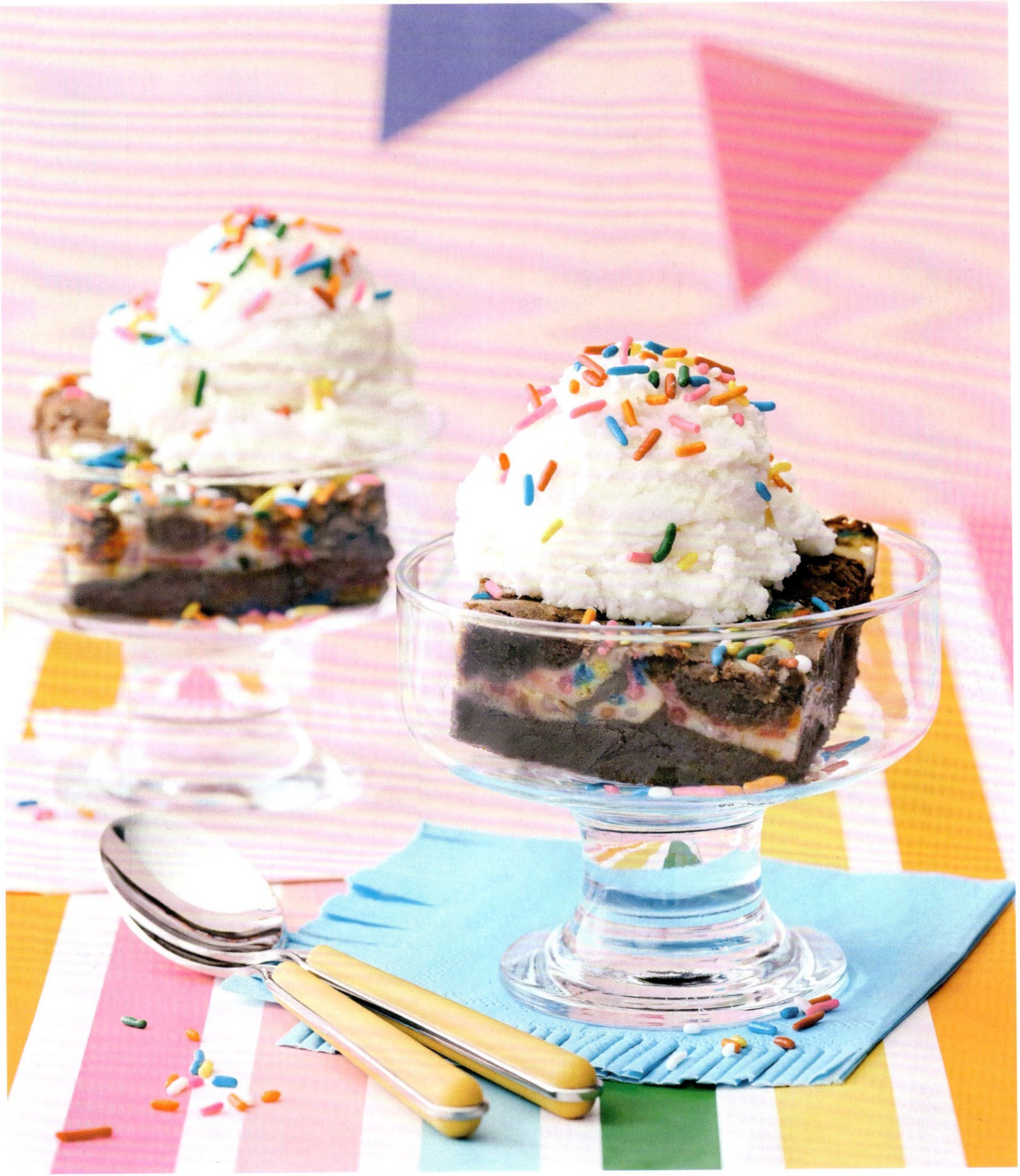

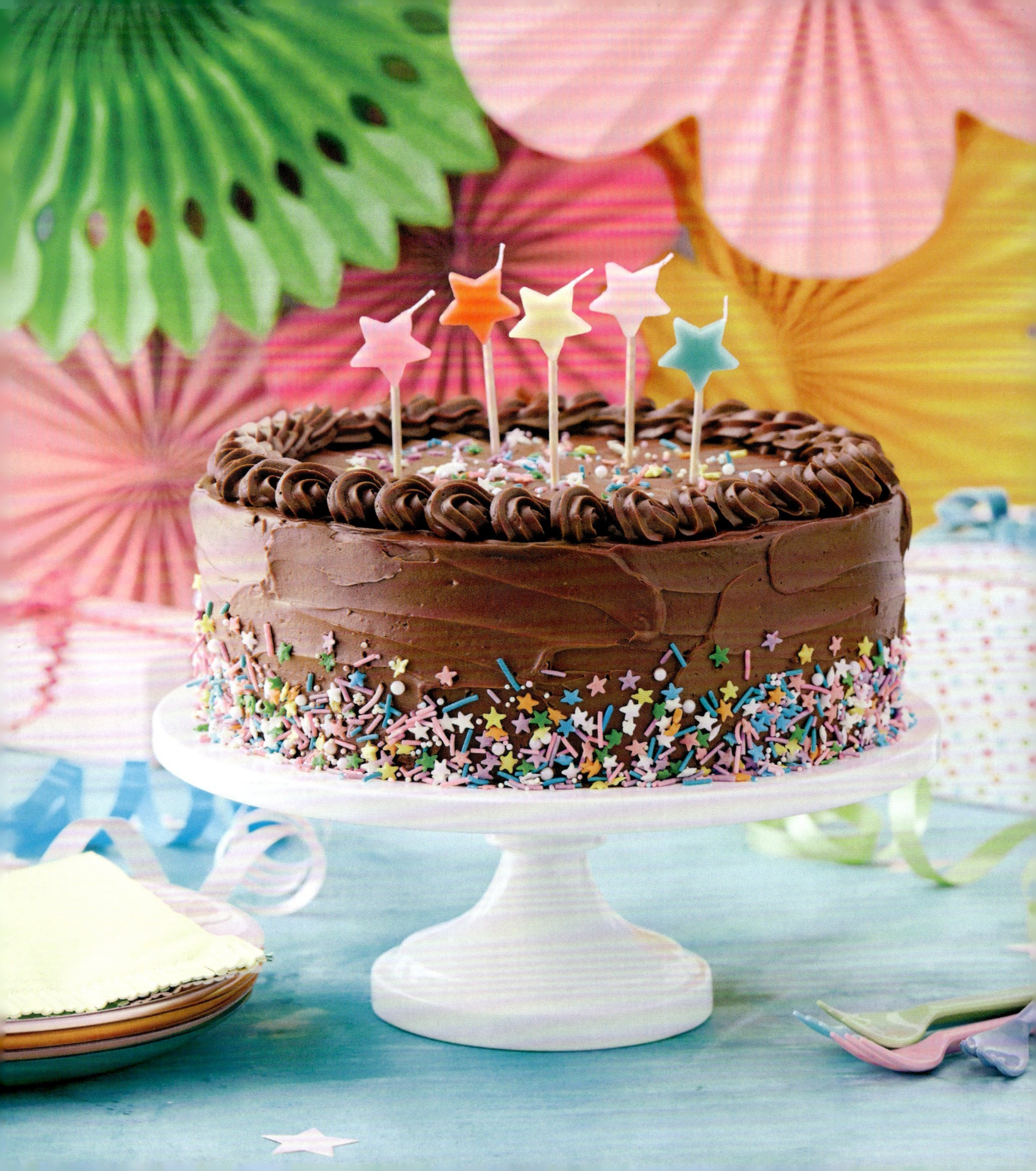

American Girl

Birthday!

Cakes, Cupcakes & Specialty Treats

weldon**owen**

Contents

BIRTHDAY TIME! *7*

Cakes

19
Milk Chocolate Layer Cake

20
Double Vanilla Ombré Cake

22
Vanilla Confetti Birthday Cake

26
Chocolate Peanut Butter Bundt Cake

28
Glazed Almond-Poppy Seed Mini Bundt Cakes

31
Chocolate Chip Chiffon Cake with Bananas and Caramel

34
Angel Food Strawberries and Cream Cake

36
Chocolate Mocha Dirt Sheet Cake

38
Tres Leches Cake

41
Lemon Meringue Layer Cake

43
Eight-Layer Honey Pistachio Cake

45
Berries and Cream Roulade

48
Vanilla Bean Cheesecake with Fresh Fruit

Cupcakes

53
Rainbow Glitter Cupcakes

57
Chocolate Chip Cookie Dough Cupcakes

59
Cookies and Cream Cupcakes

60
Ice Cream Cone Cupcakes

63
Choco-Mallow Cupcakes

64
Devil's Food Cupcakes

65
Mini Mint-Chocolate Chip Cupcakes

66
Coconut-Lime Cupcakes

69
Mini Red Velvet Cupcakes with Cream Cheese Frosting

70
Blackberry Cheesecake Cupcakes

Frozen Treats

75
Dulce de Leche Ice Cream Pie

76
Ice Cream Sandwiches

79
Any-Kind-of-Ice-Cream Birthday Cake

81
Profiteroles with Ice Cream and Chocolate Sauce

85
Chocolate-Caramel Brownie Ice Cream Sundaes

86
Chocolate-Mint Mini Ice Cream Cakes

87
Dreamy Orange and Vanilla Ice-Cream Pops

88
Watermelon-Mint Ice Pops

Pies and Tarts

93
S'mores Tartlets

94
Strawberry Mousse Pie

97
Chocolate Raspberry Tartlets

99
Little Cherry Galettes

102
Tropical Fruit Cream Tart

104
Spiced Apple Rose Tartlets with Caramel

107
Peach Slab Pie

110
Banana Chocolate Cream Pie

Specialty Sweets

114
Birthday Cake Brownies

117
Chocolate-Glazed Doughnut Hole Cone Cake

119
Strawberries and Cream Puffs

120
Cinnamon-Sugar Churros with Chocolate Sauce

123
Fruit and Cream Parfaits with Vanilla Shortbread

125
Raspberry-Swirled Pavlovas

128
Millionaire's Shortbread

131
Unicorn Rainbow Doughnuts

132
Chocolate Mousse Cups

133
Rainbow Rice Crispy Pops

Basic Recipes

136
Vanilla Frosting

139
Meringue Frosting

140
Cream Cheese Frosting

140
Whipped Cream

143
Dark Chocolate Frosting

143
Milk Chocolate Frosting

144
Chocolate Glaze

144
Vanilla Glaze

145
Chocolate Sauce

145
Lemon Curd

146
Strawberry "Roses"

149
Flaky Pie Dough

149
Tart Dough

INDEX 150

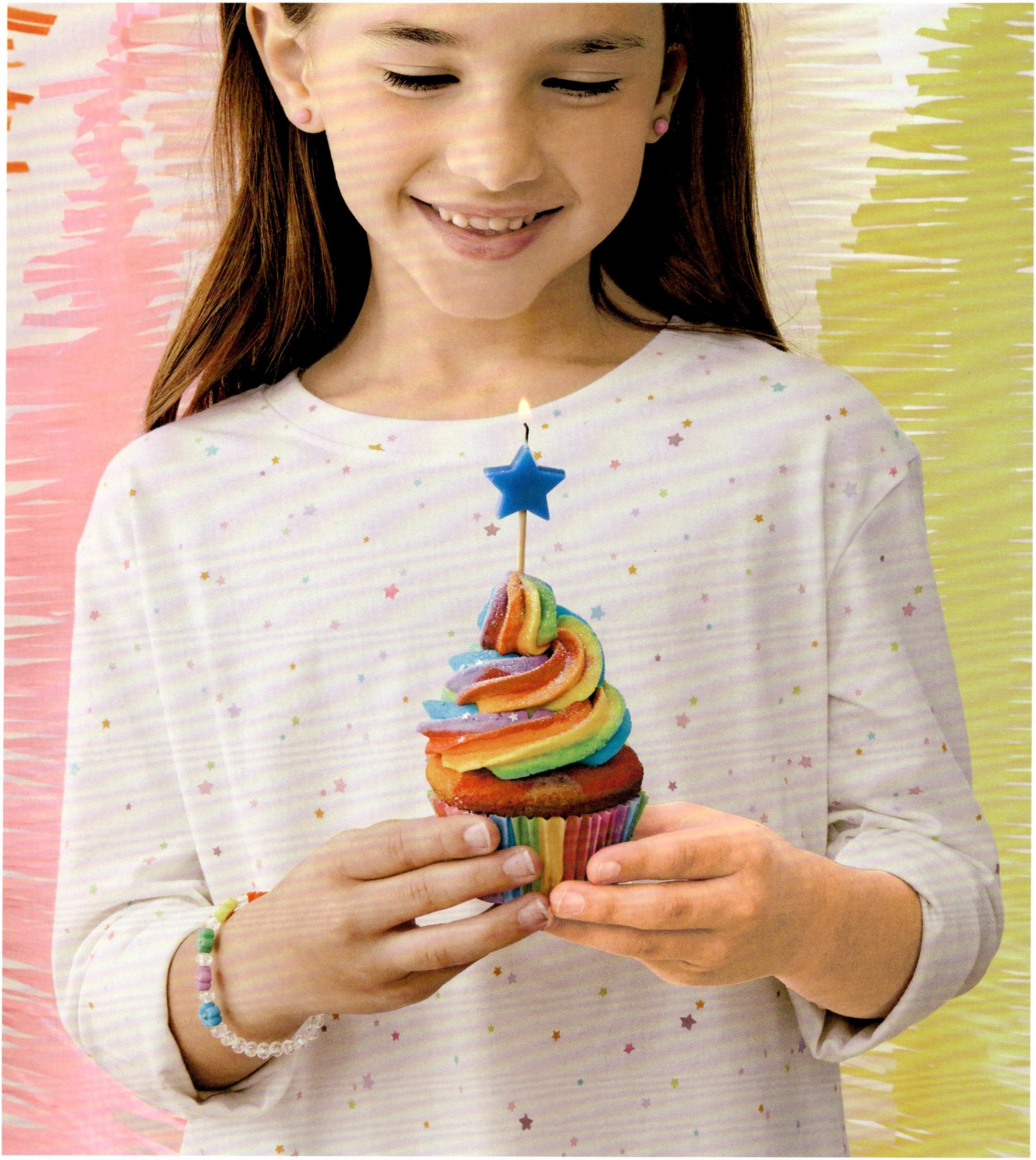

Birthday Time!

Everyone has a birthday to celebrate, and who doesn't love an awesome party? And every birthday includes cake, cookies, cupcakes, or pie—and plenty of ice cream. Sweet treats, colorful decorations, friends and family, and lots of fun are hallmarks of any birthday celebration. Whether your birthday falls in winter, spring, summer, or fall, there are countless way to mark your special day.

Each of the recipes in this book is perfect for a birthday anytime of the year. Whether you love confetti cake, chocolate tartlets, frozen treats, or glittery cupcakes, you'll find it in these pages. You'll also find lots of festive ideas to make sure your birthday party is the best time ever.

Make It Special

In these pages, you'll find lots of recipes for making birthday parties special. While the sweet treats are the centerpiece of the celebration, there are many ways to add personality to your party. You can start with a simple theme—rainbows, beach, afternoon tea, garden time, stars and stripes, ballerina, cowgirl, Hollywood—and take it from there. Have fun with color and mix and match themes, games, decorations, and/or goodie bags that add your own style. Get creative! You can decorate your cake or cupcakes to match the occasion, or even have guests add their own touch and taste with a do-it-yourself ice cream sundae or cupcake frosting bar. The most important thing to remember is to have fun! Whatever your birthday party approach—charming and cozy or bright and splashy—small special touches will make it a memorable bash.

Baking with care

When you see this symbol in the book, it means that you might need an adult to help you with all or part of the recipe. Adults have lots of culinary wisdom, and they can help keep you safe in the kitchen, where there are many hot surfaces and sharp objects. So when you are ready to begin baking, ask an adult to assist you. Also, be sure to wash your hands before you start to work.

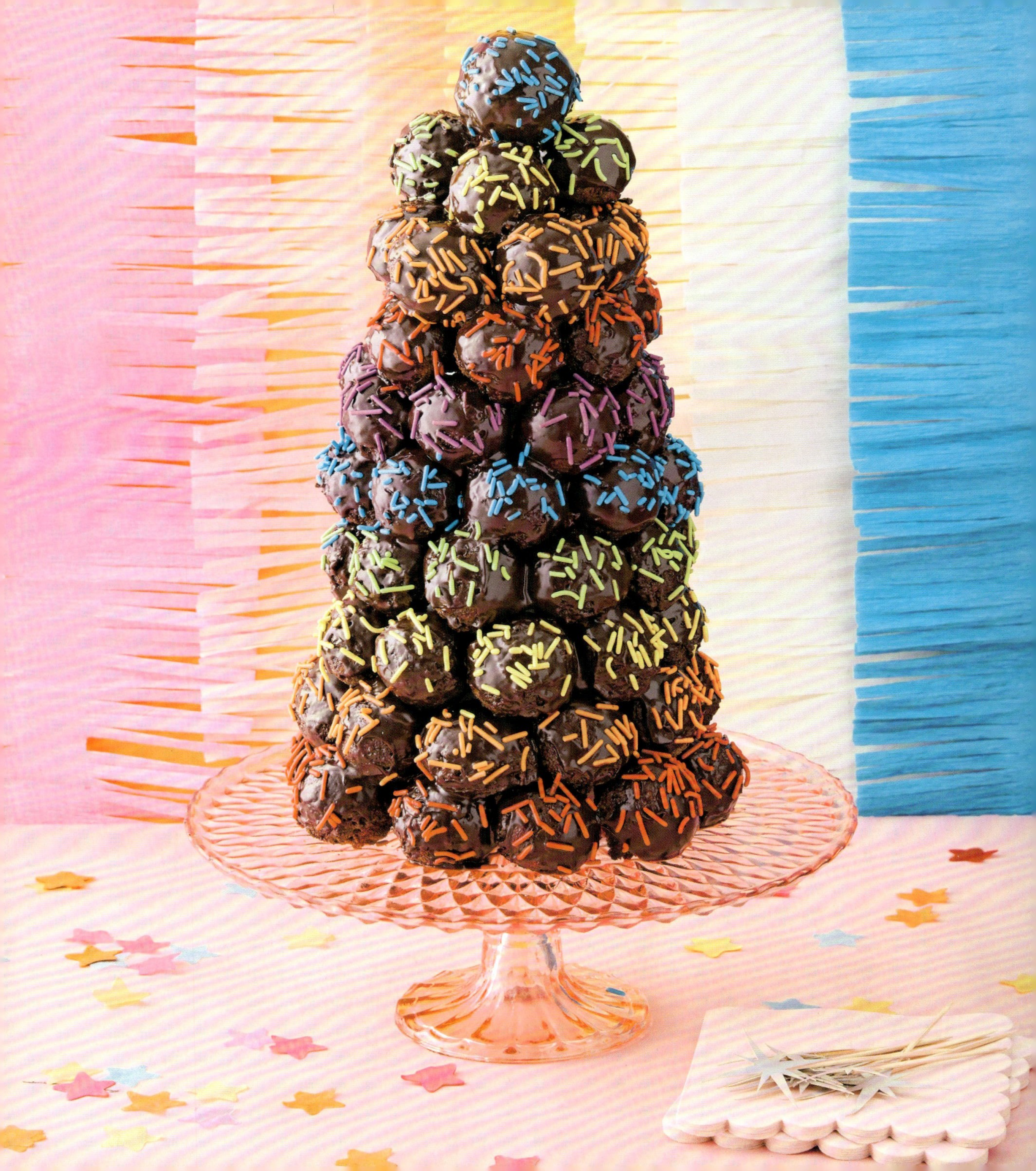

All-star baking tips

Many of the recipes in this book use an electric mixer to mix ingredients together. Hand mixers are convenient and easy to use, but you could use a stand mixer as well. Turn off the mixer before adding more ingredients and scrape down the bowl with a rubber spatula to keep any mess to a minimum and to make sure the ingredients are evenly incorporated.

Many of the recipes call for room-temperature butter because softened butter is easier to mix with other ingredients. Room-temperature eggs will mix into a batter more evenly, too, but their temperature is not critical for the recipe to work properly.

Some ingredients need to be folded into the batter instead of beaten with a mixer. When combining two mixtures of different consistencies, folding helps blend them without deflating the batter. Use a rubber spatula for this task.

In most cases, when you think your cake or cupcakes are done, stick a clean toothpick into the center. If it comes out clean, the cake or cupcakes are ready. If it comes out with batter on it, they need more baking time.

Be sure to wait for your cakes and cupcakes to cool completely before you frost them. If you don't, the frosting can melt into the top or drip off the sides.

The tools you'll need

The recipes in this book use a few basic baking tools.

★ **Measuring cups and spoons** help you measure ingredients accurately and easily. Choose graduated sets for dry ingredients and a liquid pitcher for wet ingredients.

★ **Rubber spatulas, whisks, and wooden spoons** are helpful for mixing batters and folding ingredients, food coloring, and sprinkles into batters and frostings.

★ **An electric mixer** is handy for making batters and frostings and for beating egg whites and cream.

★ **Oven mitts or pads** protect your hands from hot cake pans, muffin pans, baking sheets, and oven racks.

★ **An ice cream scoop** is helpful for dividing batter evenly among the cups of a muffin pan.

★ **A piping bag and pastry tips** are essential for adding some frostings and for decorating (page 13).

★ **Offset spatulas in a couple of sizes** are good for spreading frosting on cakes and cupcakes and transferring hot baked goods to a wire rack.

★ **Rimmed cookie sheets** are useful for transporting tartlets, galettes, individual cakes and pavlovas, and other small treats to and from the oven; baking cookies; toasting coconut; and many other baking tasks.

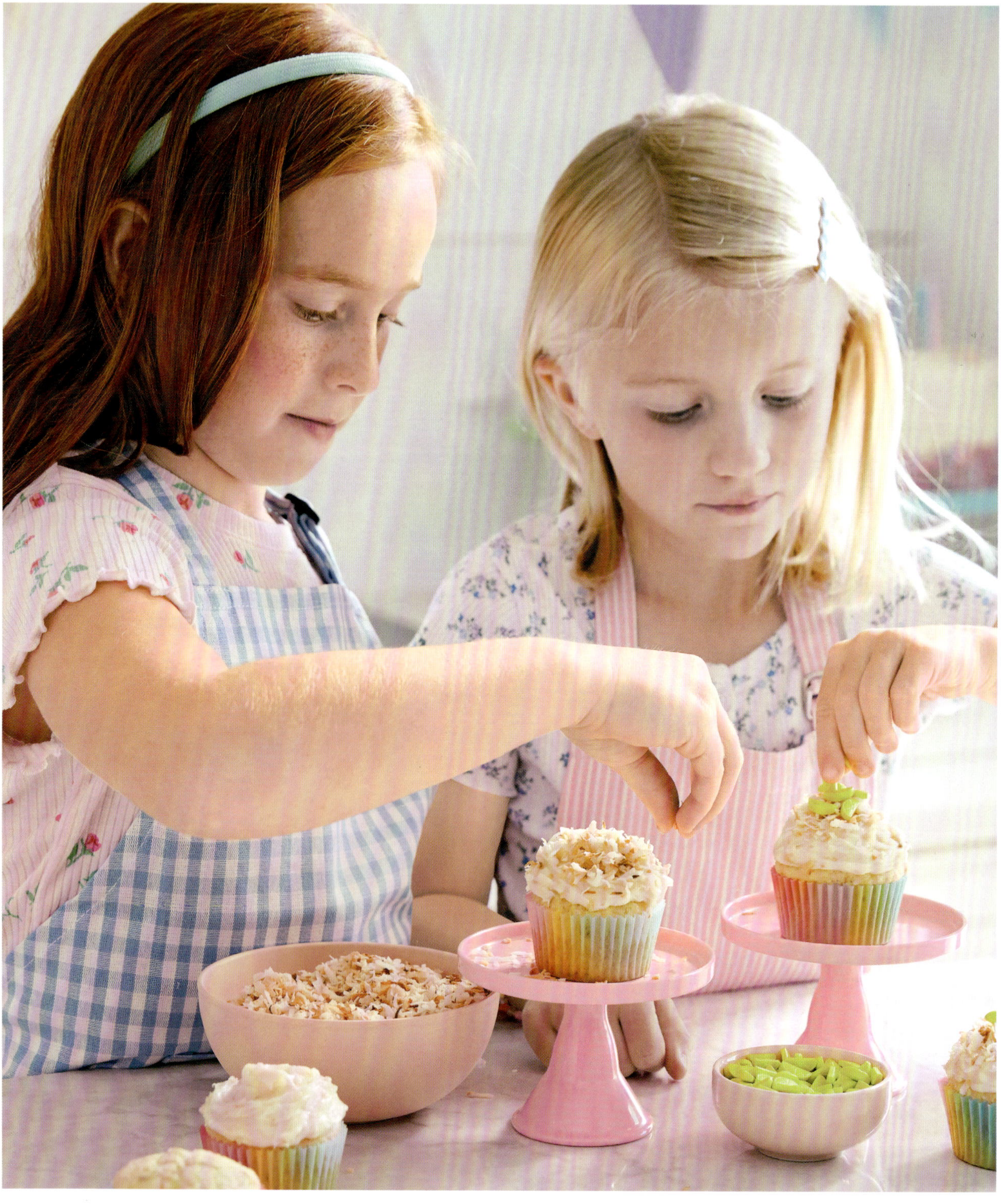

Birthday cake & cupcake decorating 101

The best part of cake and cupcake making is decorating. Gather an assortment of sprinkles, colorful liners, and food coloring for lots of creativity and fun.

★ **Sprinkles** come in all different shapes, colors, and sizes. We provide suggestions for which to use in many recipes, but let your imagination run wild, get creative, and choose whatever you like. You can make it personal by using the birthday girl's favorite color, or you can choose shades that match the party theme and decorations. Keep in mind that some sprinkles bleed when added to batter, so be careful when folding them in.

★ **Cupcake liners** are available in a variety of colors and patterns. For a birthday celebration, match your liners to the colors in your frosting and/or sprinkles.

★ A **piping bag** fitted with a **pastry tip** is a fun and pretty way to add frosting or to write fun messages on top of cakes, cupcakes, and cookies. Piping tips for pastry bags come in many shapes and sizes. Each tip is labeled with a number—the smaller the number, the smaller the hole. It's useful to have at least one plain and one star-shaped tip on hand to create different decorations.

To fill a pastry bag, firmly push a piping tip down into the small hole at the bottom of the bag. Form a cuff by folding down the top one-third of the bag. Place one hand under the cuff. Using a rubber spatula, scoop the frosting into the bag with your other hand, filling the bag halfway. Unfold the cuff, push the frosting down toward the tip, and twist the bag closed where the frosting ends. Squeeze the bag from the top when you pipe. If you'd like to use the same frosting to pipe different shapes, use a coupler attachment on your piping bag so you can change tips easily.

Birthdays are all about fun, friends, special sweet treats—and plenty of ice cream!

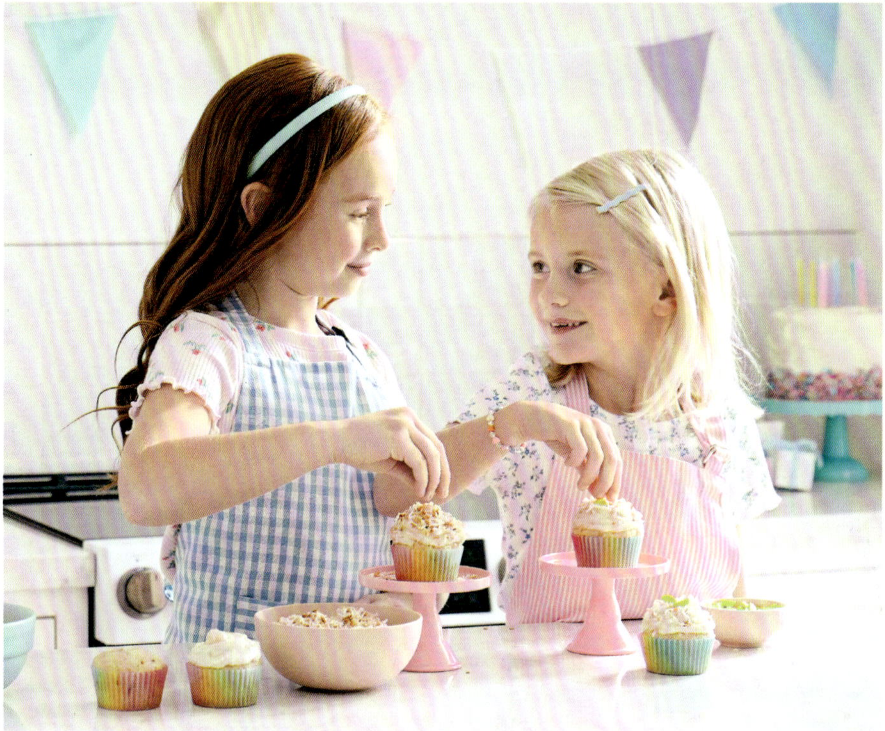

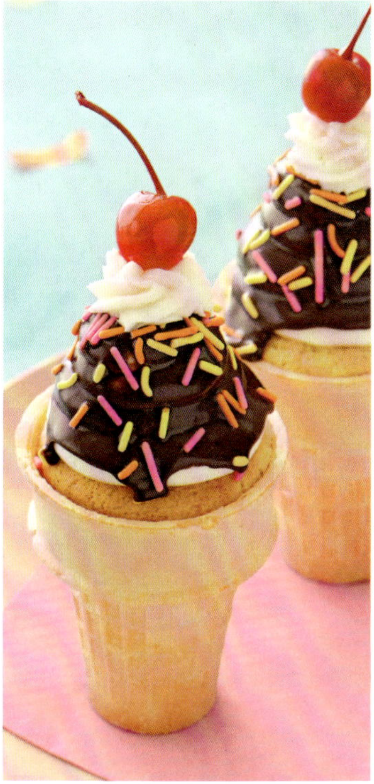

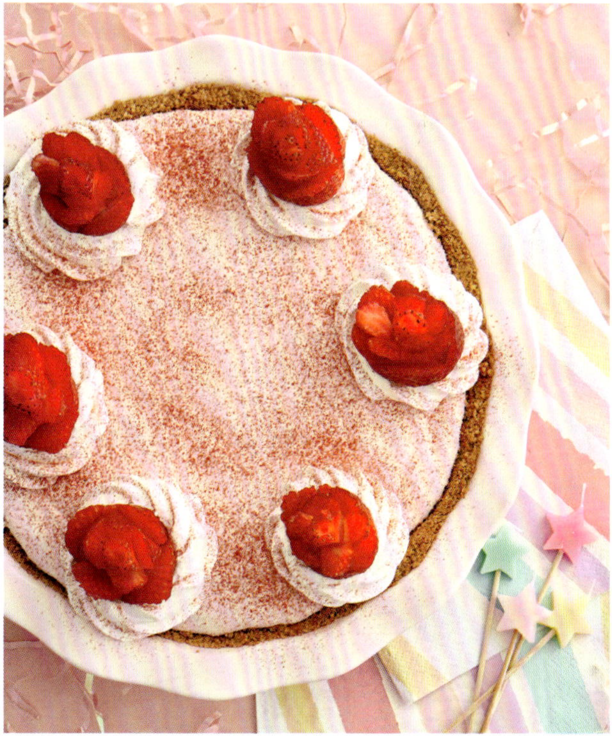

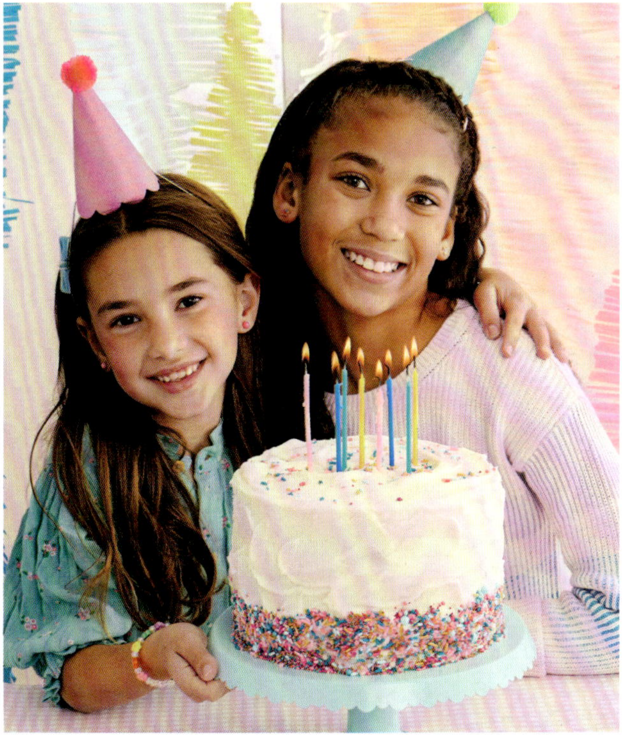

Cakes

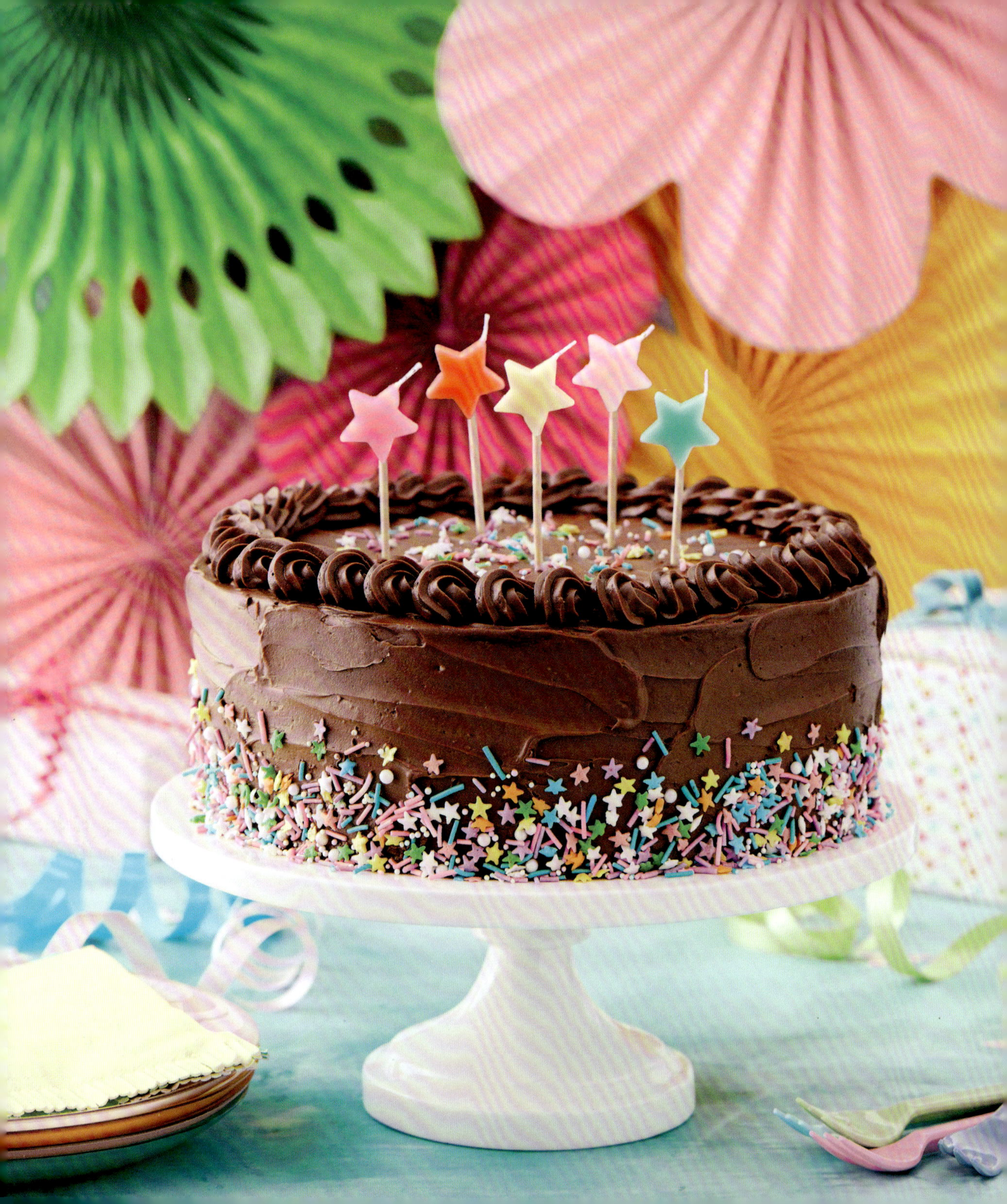

Milk Chocolate Layer Cake

The ultimate cake for all chocolate lovers! Use a good-quality milk chocolate, ideally one that is at least 40 percent cacao. The sprinkles take this all-chocolate treat over the top.

MAKES 10–12 SERVINGS

½ cup (1 stick) unsalted butter, at room temperature, plus more for the pans

2 cups all-purpose flour, plus more for the pans

6 ounces milk chocolate, chopped

½ cup water

⅔ cup unsweetened natural cocoa powder

1 cup whole milk

2 teaspoons baking powder

½ teaspoon baking soda

1 teaspoon salt

1½ cups sugar

¼ cup canola oil

3 large eggs, at room temperature

2 teaspoons vanilla extract

Milk Chocolate Frosting (page 143)

Chocolate sprinkles or sprinkles of choice, for decorating

Preheat the oven to 350°F. Lightly butter the bottoms and sides of two 9-inch round cake pans, line the bottoms with parchment paper, and butter the parchment. Dust the pans with flour, tapping out the excess.

In a saucepan over medium-low heat, melt the milk chocolate with the water, whisking until smooth. Sift the cocoa powder into the mixture and whisk to combine. Whisk in the milk until smooth and set aside to cool.

In a medium bowl, whisk together the flour, baking powder, baking soda, and salt. In a large bowl, using an electric mixer, beat together the butter, sugar, and oil on medium speed until light and fluffy, about 2 minutes. Beat in the eggs one at a time, beating after each addition until incorporated. Add the vanilla and beat until blended. Stop the mixer and scrape down the bowl with a rubber spatula. On low speed, add the cooled chocolate and beat until mixed. Add the flour mixture and beat until incorporated, stopping to scrape down the bowl as needed.

Divide the batter between the prepared pans and smooth the tops. Bake the layers until a toothpick inserted into the center of a layer comes out clean, about 30 minutes. Let cool on wire racks for 15 minutes, then invert the cakes onto the racks, lift off the pans, peel off the parchment, and let cool completely.

To assemble, place a cake layer on a serving plate. Using an offset spatula, spread one-third of the frosting evenly over the top. Place the second layer on top and spread half of the remaining frosting over the top and sides with sprinkles. If you have extra frosting, pipe a pretty border around the top.

Double Vanilla Ombré Cake

Gradations of pink from light to dark make this magnificent cake look as if it came straight out of a bakery. Nearly any color will work—blue or purple would also be stunning—so choose food coloring in a hue that that suits the birthday girl. The cakes can be baked a day ahead, wrapped tightly in plastic wrap, and stored at room temperature, making day-of assembly a snap.

MAKES 10–12 SERVINGS

¾ cup (1½ sticks) unsalted butter, at room temperature, plus more for the pans

2¾ cups all-purpose flour, plus more for the pans

2½ teaspoons baking powder

¾ teaspoon baking soda

¾ teaspoon salt

3 large egg whites, plus 1 large whole egg

2 cups sugar

1 tablespoon vanilla extract

1½ cups buttermilk

Pink, red, or other gel food coloring of choice

6 cups Vanilla Frosting (page 136)

Position 2 oven racks in the center of the oven and preheat the oven to 350°F. Butter the bottoms and sides of four 8-inch round cake pans, line the bottoms with parchment paper, and butter the parchment. Dust the pans with flour, tapping out the excess.

In a medium bowl, sift together the flour, baking powder, baking soda, and salt. In a stand mixer fitted with the whisk attachment, beat together the egg whites and 1 cup of the sugar on medium-high speed until soft peaks form, about 4 minutes.

In a clean bowl of the stand mixer fitted with the paddle attachment, beat together the butter and the remaining 1 cup sugar on medium speed until pale and fluffy, about 2 minutes. Add the whole egg and vanilla and beat until blended, about 1 minute. Stop the mixer and scrape down bowl with a rubber spatula. On low speed, add the flour mixture in three additions alternately with the buttermilk in two additions, beginning and ending with the flour mixture and beating just until blended after each addition. Stop the mixer and scrape down the bowl. Then beat the batter on high speed for 20 seconds.

Using the rubber spatula, pile one-fourth of the egg whites on top of the batter and fold them in to lighten the mixture. Then pile the remaining egg whites on top and gently fold them in just until no white streaks remain.

Divide the batter evenly among 4 medium bowls. Add food coloring to 3 of the bowls, making light, medium, and dark shades of the same color. Gently fold in the food coloring until the batter in each bowl is evenly colored. Leave 1 bowl of batter plain.

Pour each batter into a prepared pan and spread evenly. Bake the cake layers, rotating the pans between the racks halfway through baking, until a toothpick inserted into the center of a cake comes out clean, 15–20 minutes. Let cool in the pans on wire racks for 10 minutes, then invert the cakes onto the racks, lift off the pans, peel off the parchment, and let cool completely.

Set aside half of the frosting for the filling, crumb coat, and first row of rosettes. Spoon half of the remaining frosting into a bowl, then add food coloring to make it the darkest shade of the batter colors. Divide the remaining frosting between 2 bowls. Add food coloring to the bowls to make the light and medium shades. Stir the frosting in each bowl until evenly colored.

To assemble the cake, place the plain cake layer on a serving plate. Using an offset spatula, spread about ¼ cup of the plain frosting evenly over the cake, then top with the lightest dyed cake layer. Spread it with about ¼ cup of the plain frosting and top with medium dyed cake layer. Spread it with about ¼ cup of the plain frosting and top with the darkest dyed cake layer. Then spread a very thin layer of plain frosting over the top and sides of the cake (this is the crumb coat). Refrigerate the cake until you are ready to pipe the rosettes.

Spoon the remaining plain frosting into a piping bag fitted with a large closed star tip. Starting at the base of the cake, pipe a single row of rosettes around the cake. Working directly above the first row, repeat with the lightest-colored frosting (using a clean piping bag and tip), followed by a row made from the medium-colored frosting. Finally, pipe the darkest shade in a single row of rosettes around the cake and then pipe rosettes all over the top of the cake. Serve right away.

Vanilla Confetti Birthday Cake

This triple-layer cake is ready for a party. Classic vanilla butter cake is brightened up with flecks of rainbow sprinkles. Use jimmies or nonpareils; either one works great. Or try your own color scheme with your favorite sprinkles.

MAKES 10–12 SERVINGS

1 cup (2 sticks) unsalted butter, at room temperature, plus more for the pans

3¼ cups all-purpose flour, plus more for the pans

1 tablespoon baking powder

1 teaspoon baking soda

½ teaspoon salt

¾ cup water

¾ cup whole milk

½ cup buttermilk

1¾ cups sugar

1 tablespoon vanilla extract

3 large eggs

2 cups rainbow sprinkles

Vanilla Frosting (page 136)

Preheat the oven to 325°F. Lightly butter the bottoms and sides of three 8-inch round cake pans, line the bottoms with parchment paper, and butter the parchment. Dust the pans with flour, tapping out the excess.

In a large bowl, sift together the flour, baking powder, baking soda, and salt. In a large liquid measuring cup, whisk together the water, milk, and buttermilk.

In a stand mixer fitted with the paddle attachment, beat the butter on medium speed until smooth and creamy, about 3 minutes. Add the sugar and vanilla and beat until pale and fluffy, about 2 minutes. Add the eggs one at a time, beating after each addition until incorporated. On low speed, add the flour mixture in four additions alternately with the milk mixture in three additions, beginning and ending with the flour mixture and beating just until blended after each addition. Stop the mixer after each addition to scrape down the bowl with a rubber spatula.

Remove the bowl from the mixer stand and, using the rubber spatula, gently fold in 1 cup of the sprinkles. Divide the batter evenly among the prepared pans and smooth the tops.

Continued on page 25

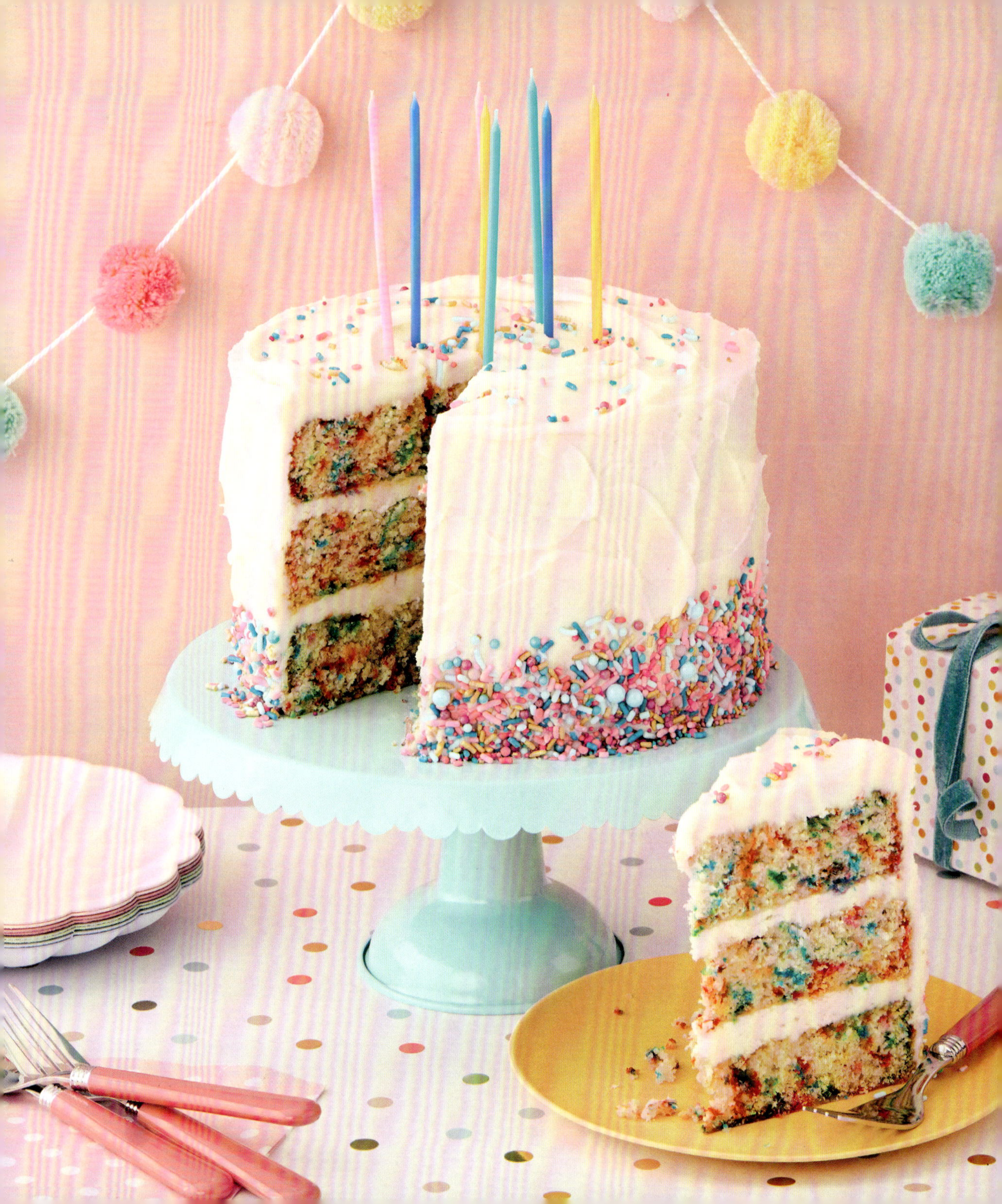

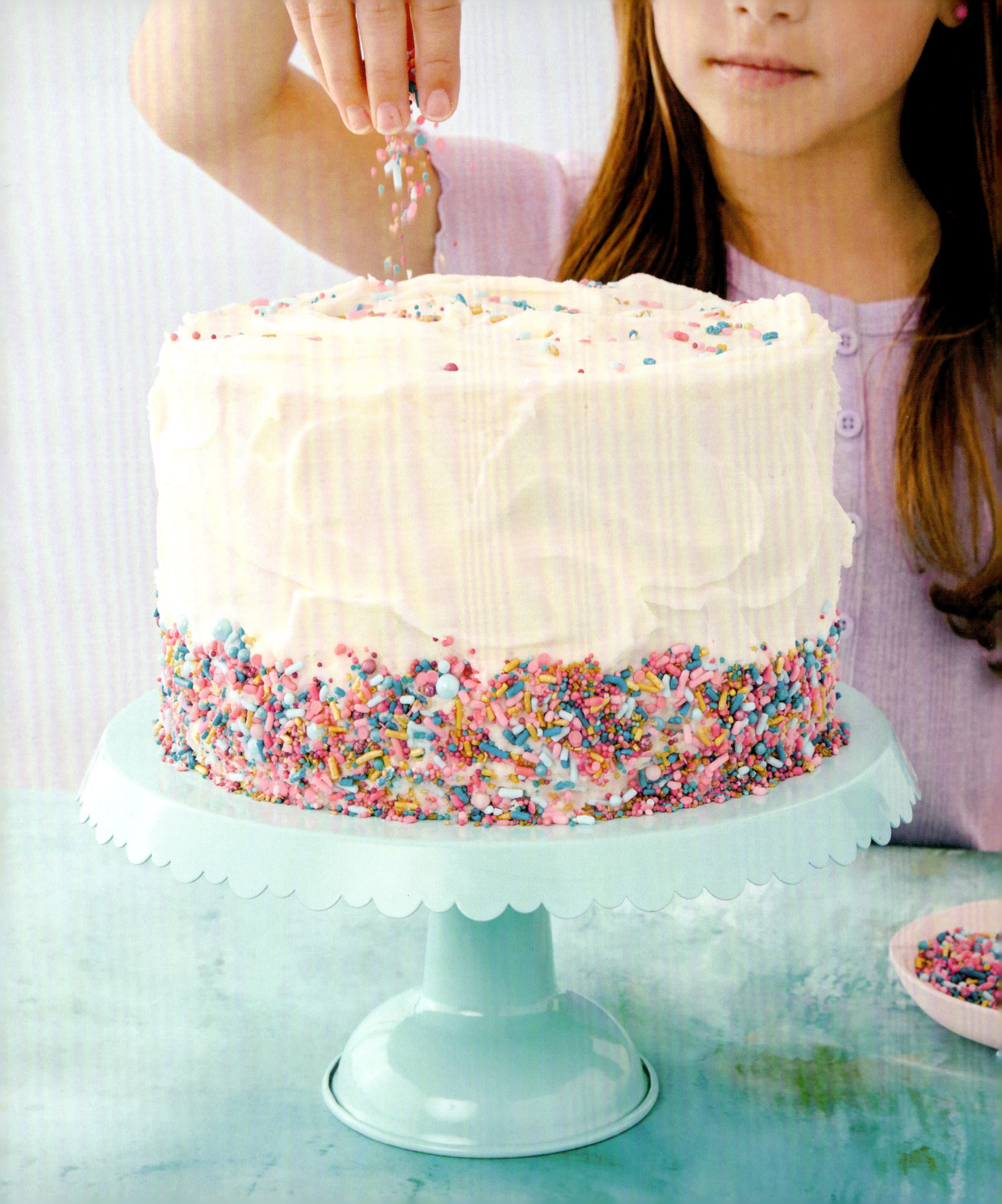

> **Party Showstopper!**
> For a special display, serve the confetti cake on a pretty pedestal; decorate the base with ribbons, flowers, or little presents that tie in with the party theme and colors.

~ *Continued from page 22* ~

Bake the cake layers until a toothpick inserted into the center of a layer comes out clean, about 40 minutes. Let cool in the pans on wire racks for 20 minutes. Then run a thin knife along the inside edge of each pan to loosen the cake, invert the cakes onto the racks, lift off the pans, and peel off the parchment. Let cool completely. Turn the cake layers right side up and, using a long serrated knife, trim off the rounded top of each layer so the top is flat.

To assemble the cake, place a cake layer, top side up, on a serving plate. Using an offset spatula, spread a thick layer of the frosting over the top. Place a second layer, top side up, on the frosting layer and spread a thick layer of frosting over the top. Repeat with the third layer, spreading the remaining frosting in a thick layer over the top and around the sides of the cake. Decorate the tops and sides with the remaining 1 cup sprinkles.

Serve right away, or to store, place in a cake keeper or cover tightly with plastic wrap (use toothpicks to tent the plastic wrap away from the frosted surface) and refrigerate for up to 2 days.

Chocolate Peanut Butter Bundt Cake

The perfect collision of dark chocolate and peanut butter, this dense cake is for everyone who can't get enough of the popular flavor combo. Here, peanut butter and chocolate batters are swirled together and baked in a Bundt pan, and then the cooled cake is finished with a rich chocolate glaze and decorated with plenty of roasted peanuts and peanut butter cups. Divine!

MAKES 10–12 SERVINGS

Unsalted butter and all-purpose flour, for the pan

FOR THE PEANUT BUTTER BATTER

1 cup creamy natural peanut butter (unsweetened)

1 cup sugar

4 tablespoons (½ stick) unsalted butter, at room temperature

1 large egg

1 teaspoon vanilla extract

½ teaspoon salt

¼ cup sour cream

1¼ cups all-purpose flour

1 teaspoon baking powder

¼ teaspoon baking soda

Preheat the oven to 350°F. Generously butter a 10-cup Bundt pan, then dust with flour, tapping out the excess.

To make the peanut butter batter, in a medium bowl, using an electric mixer, beat together the peanut butter, sugar, and butter on medium speed until well mixed and creamy, about 1 minute. Add the egg, vanilla, salt, and sour cream and beat until smooth. In a second medium bowl, whisk together the flour, baking powder, and baking soda. Add the flour mixture to the peanut butter mixture and stir just until well mixed. The batter will be thick. Set aside.

To make the chocolate batter, in a saucepan over low heat, melt the chocolate and butter with the oil, stirring with a whisk until smooth. Add the cocoa powder and stir until smooth. Add the sugar, sour cream, egg, and vanilla and whisk until smooth. In a large bowl, whisk together the flour, baking powder, baking soda, and salt. Add the chocolate mixture to the flour mixture and stir just until well mixed. The batter will be thick.

Using a large spoon, dollop the peanut butter batter and the chocolate batter alternately into the prepared pan. Using a table knife, swirl the batters together slightly as best you can and smooth the batter into an even layer.

FOR THE CHOCOLATE BATTER

4 ounces bittersweet chocolate, finely chopped

4 tablespoons (½ stick) unsalted butter

¼ cup canola oil

¼ cup unsweetened natural cocoa powder

1 cup sugar

½ cup sour cream

1 large egg

1 teaspoon vanilla extract

1 cup all-purpose flour

1 teaspoon baking powder

¼ teaspoon baking soda

¼ teaspoon salt

Chocolate Glaze (page 144)

Mini chocolate peanut butter cups and/or chopped roasted peanuts, for decorating (optional)

Bake the cake until a toothpick inserted near the center comes out clean, 60–65 minutes. Let cool in the pan on a wire rack for about 15 minutes, then invert the cake onto the rack, lift off the pan, and let cool completely.

Line the bottom of a rimmed baking sheet with parchment paper. Set a wire rack on the lined pan and place the cake on the rack. Slowly pour the glaze over the top of the cake, covering it completely and letting it run down the sides. Let set for about 20 minutes. If you prefer a thicker glaze, scrape up the glaze from the parchment, transfer it to a bowl, and glaze the cake a second time, then let set again. Slide the cake onto a serving platter. Decorate with peanut butter cups and roasted peanuts, if you like. Serve, cut into wedges.

Make It Fancy!
Try this recipe with almond or hazelnut butter and/or cover the cake with chocolate shavings for an over-the-top birthday treat.

Glazed Almond-Poppy Seed Mini Bundt Cakes

These little Bundt cakes are extra cute and extra lemony! If you don't have mini Bundt pans, you can bake the cake batter in a standard or jumbo muffin pan and then glaze the cakes as directed. Edible flowers, like violas or nasturtiums, are an easy and beautiful way to decorate these poppy seed–speckled cakes.

MAKES 6 INDIVIDUAL CAKES

FOR THE CAKES

½ cup (1 stick) plus 2 tablespoons unsalted butter, at cool room temperature, cut into tablespoon-size pieces, plus more at room temperature for the molds

⅓ cup all-purpose flour, plus more for the molds

1 tablespoon poppy seeds

½ teaspoon baking powder

¼ teaspoon salt

5 ounces almond paste, broken into small pieces

⅔ cup granulated sugar

2 teaspoons finely grated lemon zest

3 large eggs, at room temperature

1 teaspoon vanilla extract

Preheat the oven to 350°F. Generously butter 6 mini Bundt molds (each about ¾-cup capacity). Dust them with flour, tapping out the excess.

To make the cakes, in a small bowl, whisk together the flour, poppy seeds, baking powder, and salt. In a large bowl, using an electric mixer, beat together the almond paste, sugar, and lemon zest on low speed until the almond paste breaks down and a crumbly mixture has formed, about 3 minutes. Increase the speed to medium-high and add the butter a few pieces at a time, beating until the mixture is well blended, pale, and fluffy, about 2 minutes. Stop the mixer and scrape down the bowl with a rubber spatula. On medium-high speed, add the eggs one at a time, beating after each addition until incorporated. Add the vanilla and beat until blended. Stop the mixer and scrape down the bowl. Add the flour mixture and stir by hand until fully incorporated.

Divide the batter evenly among the prepared Bundt molds, filling each one two-thirds to three-fourths full. The easiest way to do this is to spoon the batter into a piping bag fitted with a large round tip and to pipe it into the molds. Smooth the top of each mold. Arrange the filled molds on a rimmed baking sheet.

Continued on page 30

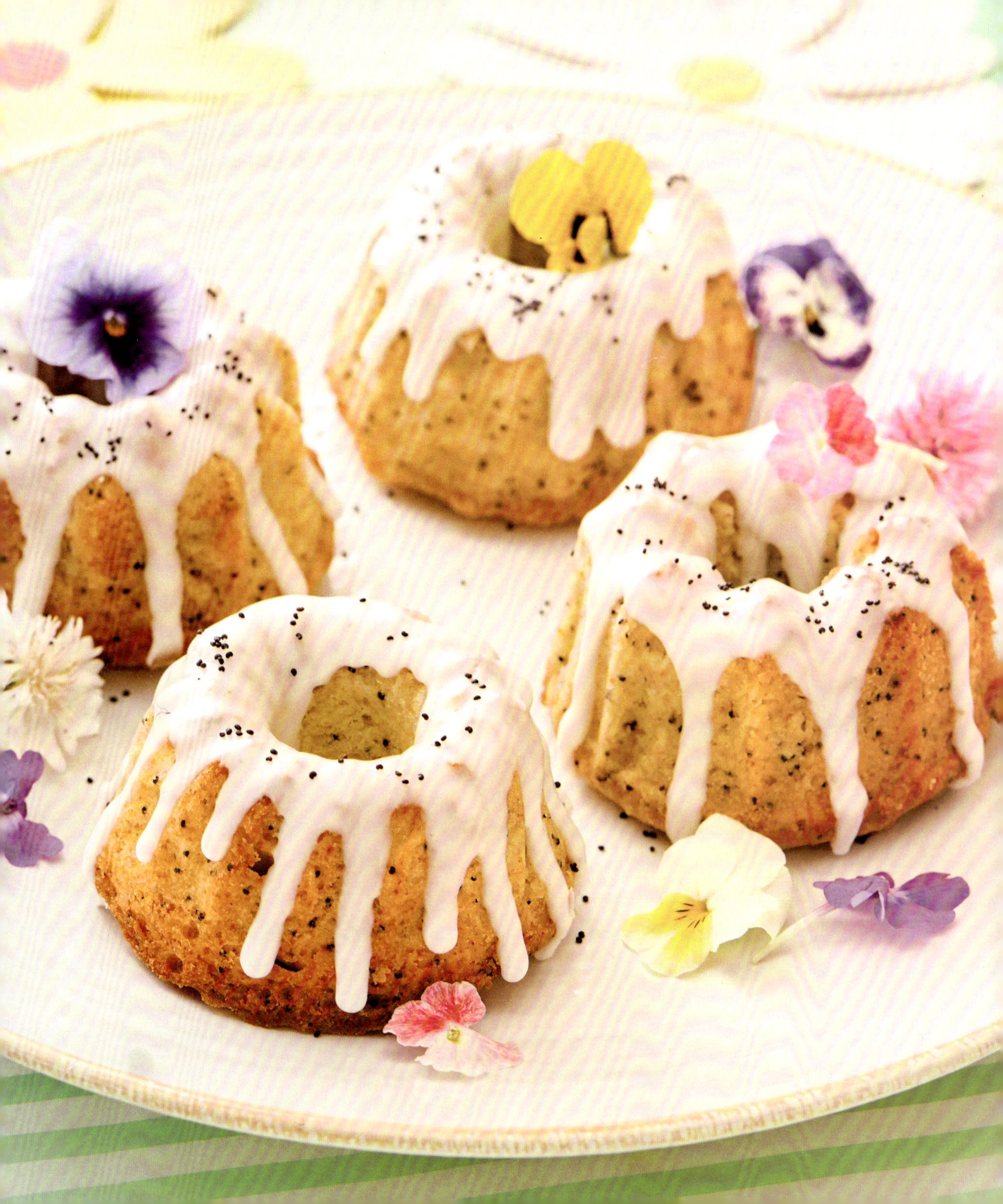

~ *Continued from page 28* ~

FOR THE LEMON GLAZE

1½ cups powdered sugar, sifted

2 tablespoons fresh lemon juice

Pinch of salt

Poppy seeds, for garnish

Small edible flowers, for decorating

Bake the cakes until a toothpick inserted into the center of each cake comes out clean, 17–20 minutes. Transfer the baking sheet to a wire rack and let the cakes cool in the molds for 10 minutes. Then invert the cakes onto the rack, lift off the molds, and let cool completely.

To make the glaze, whisk together the powdered sugar, lemon juice, and salt to form a thick but pourable glaze. Line the bottom of a rimmed baking sheet with parchment paper and set the wire rack holding the cakes on the baking sheet. Pour the glaze over the cakes, dividing it evenly and using a spoon to spread it over the edges so it drips down the sides. Decorate with a light sprinkling of poppy seeds and flowers and let set for about 10 minutes before serving.

Flower Power
Edible flowers add color, beauty, and an elegant touch to any birthday cake or cupcake. Choose from organic blooms such as nasturtium, pansies, or roses.

Chocolate Chip Chiffon Cake with Bananas and Caramel

This classic chiffon cake is leavened with a meringue and kept moist and tender with the addition of oil. The chocolate chip–studded layers are filled with caramel sauce, sliced bananas, and whipped cream. For a berry-cream cake, omit the caramel and swap out the bananas for sliced strawberries or whole raspberries.

MAKES 10–12 SERVINGS

2 cups cake flour

1 tablespoon baking powder

½ teaspoon salt

1 cup sugar

1 cup mini chocolate chips, plus more for decorating

6 large eggs, separated

½ cup canola oil

½ cup water

2 teaspoons vanilla extract

½ teaspoon cream of tartar

⅔ cup store-bought thick caramel sauce, plus more for decorating

2–3 bananas, peeled and thickly sliced, plus more slices for decorating

3 cups Whipped Cream (page 140)

Preheat the oven to 350°F. Line the bottoms of three 9-inch round cake pans with parchment paper.

In a large bowl, sift together the flour, baking powder, and salt. Whisk ½ cup of the sugar into the flour mixture, then stir in the chocolate chips. In a medium bowl, whisk together the egg yolks, oil, water, and vanilla until blended. Add the egg yolk mixture to the flour mixture and stir just until smooth.

In a large bowl, using an electric mixer, beat together the egg whites and cream of tartar on medium speed until foamy. Increase the speed to medium-high, then slowly add the remaining ½ cup sugar and continue to beat until medium-stiff peaks form. Using a rubber spatula, pile one-fourth of the egg whites on top of the batter and fold them in to lighten the mixture. Then pile the remaining egg whites on top and gently fold them in just until no white streaks remain. Divide the batter evenly among the prepared pans.

Bake the cake layers until a toothpick inserted into the center of a layer comes out clean, about 20 minutes. Let cool completely in the pans on wire racks. Run a thin knife along the inside edge of each pan to loosen the cake, invert the cakes onto the racks, lift off the pans, and peel off the parchment.

Continued on page 33

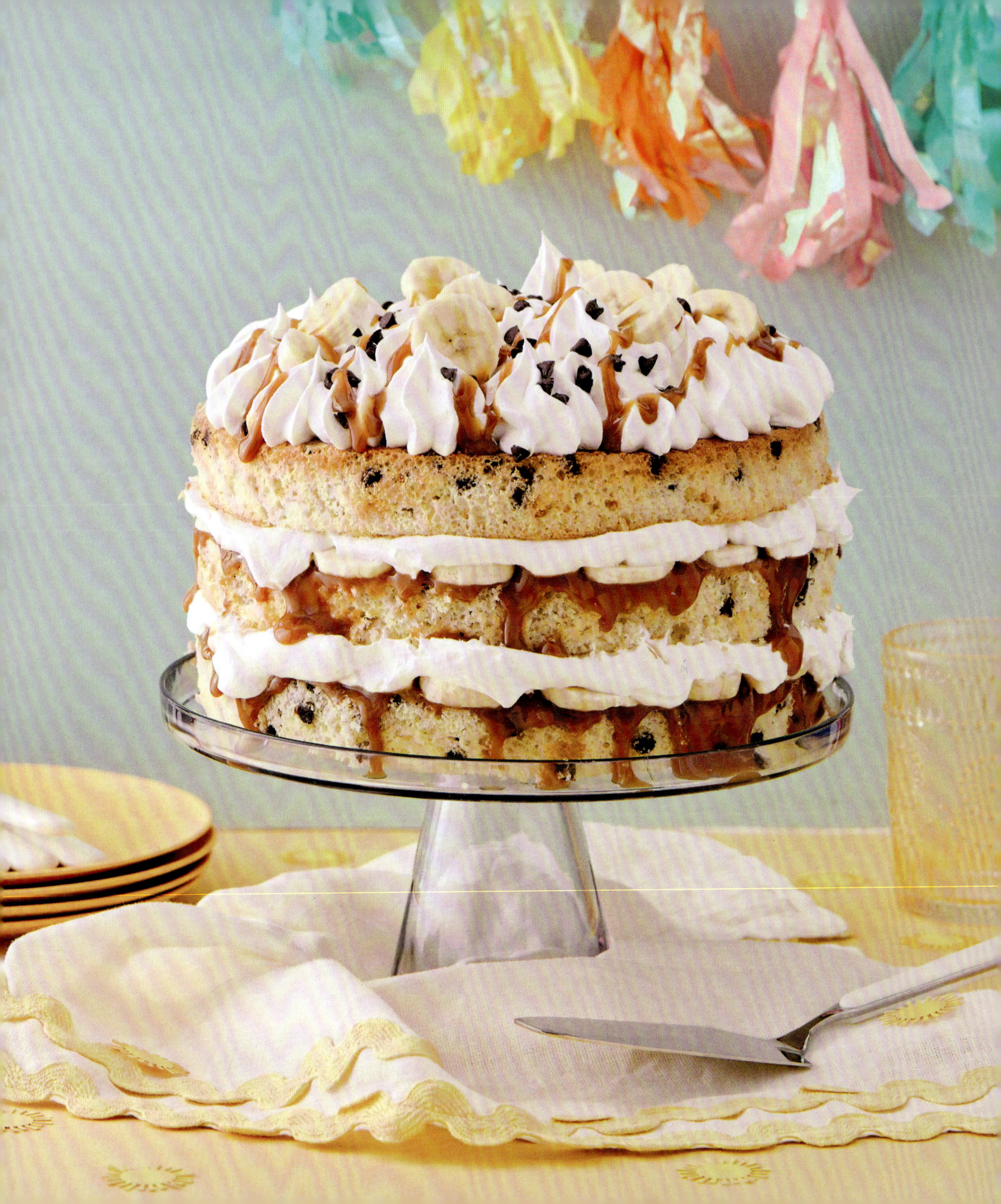

~ *Continued from page 31* ~

To assemble the cake, first check to see if the caramel sauce is spreadable. If not, transfer it to a microwave-safe bowl and warm it in the microwave on high power just until spreadable. Then place a cake layer on a serving plate. Using an offset spatula, spread half of the caramel sauce over the top. Arrange half of the banana slices in an even layer over the caramel. Wipe the offset spatula clean, then spread an even layer of the whipped cream over the banana layer. Place a second cake layer on the whipped cream layer, spread with the remaining caramel sauce, top with the remaining banana slices, and then spread an even layer of the whipped cream over the banana layer. Place the third cake layer on the whipped cream, then spread the remaining whipped cream on top. Alternatively, spoon the remaining whipped cream into a piping bag fitted with a small star tip and pipe the cream decoratively on top of the cake.

Decorate the top of the cake with chocolate chips, banana slices, and drizzles of caramel sauce. Serve right away.

Angel Food Strawberries and Cream Cake

Angel food cake gets it's loft from whipped eggs whites only, rather than baking powder or baking soda like most other cakes. Be sure to start with a clean bowl for the egg whites, and don't overwhip them or the cake will be dry.

MAKES 10–12 SERVINGS

FOR THE CAKE

1 cup all-purpose flour

1½ cups sugar

12 large egg whites, at room temperature

1 teaspoon cream of tartar

½ teaspoon salt

2 teaspoons vanilla extract

FOR THE BERRIES AND CREAM

1½ pounds strawberries, hulled and sliced

¼ cup sugar

4 cups Whipped Cream (page 140)

Preheat the oven to 325°F. Have ready an ungreased 9- or 10-inch angel food cake pan.

To make the cake, in a bowl, sift together the flour and ½ cup of the sugar. Repeat the sifting three more times.

In a stand mixer fitted with the whisk attachment, beat the egg whites on low speed until foamy, about 2 minutes. Add the cream of tartar, salt, and vanilla, increase the speed to medium, and beat until soft peaks form, about 4 minutes. With the mixer running on medium-high speed, slowly add the remaining 1 cup sugar. Then increase the speed to high and beat until stiff peaks form, about 2 minutes. Remove the bowl from the mixer stand and sprinkle the flour mixture over the egg white mixture. Using a rubber spatula, gently fold in the flour mixture, taking care not to overmix and deflate the egg whites.

Spoon the batter into the ungreased cake pan, then gently tap the pan on the counter to release any air pockets. Bake until the cake is golden brown and springs back when lightly touched, 35–45 minutes. Invert the pan onto a wire rack and let cool upside down for about 30 minutes. To release the cake from the pan, turn it right side up and run a thin knife along the inside edge of the pan and around the tube to loosen the cake. Then use the tube to pull the cake from the pan and run the knife between the base of the pan and the cake. Invert the cake onto the rack and lift away the base. Let the cake cool completely.

Fresh and Tasty
Stir chopped fresh mint into the strawberries, then decorate the finished cake with a few mint sprigs. Half-moon slices of lemon are also pretty on top.

To assemble the cake, prepare the berries and cream. In a medium bowl, stir together the strawberries and sugar. Let stand until the berries release their juices, about 15 minutes. Whip the cream.

Using a long serrated knife and a sawing motion, carefully cut the cake horizontally into three layers. Place the bottom layer, cut side up, on a serving plate. Using an offset spatula, spread one-third of the cream over the top. Spoon one-third of the strawberries evenly on the cream layer. Place the middle layer on top of the strawberries, spread half of the remaining cream on top, and top with half of the remaining strawberries in an even layer. Set the top layer, cut side down, on the strawberries, spread the remaining cream on top, and spoon the remaining strawberries evenly over the cream layer. Serve right away.

Chocolate Mocha Dirt Sheet Cake

Decorate this chocolate- and coffee-flavored sheet cake with gummy worms or even gummy bugs. You can also use candy flowers or edible flowers.

MAKES 10–12 SERVINGS

½ cup (1 stick) unsalted butter, at room temperature, plus more for the baking dish

2 cups all-purpose flour, plus more for dusting

6 ounces bittersweet chocolate, chopped

½ cup brewed coffee

⅔ cup unsweetened natural cocoa powder

2 teaspoons espresso powder (optional)

1 cup whole milk

2 teaspoons baking powder

½ teaspoon baking soda

1 teaspoon salt

1½ cups sugar

¼ cup canola oil

3 large eggs, at room temperature

2 teaspoons vanilla extract

2 cups Dark Chocolate Frosting (page 143)

2 cups chocolate wafer crumbs (see Note)

Gummy worms, for decorating

Preheat the oven to 350°F. Lightly butter the bottom and sides of a 9-by-13-inch baking dish. Dust with flour, tapping out the excess.

In a saucepan over medium-low heat, melt the chocolate with the coffee, whisking until smooth. Sift the cocoa powder into the mixture, add the espresso powder (if using), and whisk to combine. Whisk in the milk until smooth and set aside to cool.

In a medium bowl, whisk together the flour, baking powder, baking soda, and salt. In a large bowl, using an electric mixer, beat together the butter, sugar, and oil on medium speed until pale and fluffy, about 2 minutes. Add the eggs one at a time, beating after each addition until incorporated. Add the vanilla and beat until blended. Stop the mixer and scrape down the bowl with a rubber spatula. On low speed, add the cooled chocolate mixture and beat until well mixed. Finally, add the flour mixture and beat just until incorporated, stopping the mixer to scrape down the bowl as needed.

Scrape the batter into the prepared baking dish and smooth the top. Bake the cake until a toothpick inserted into the center comes out clean, about 30 minutes. Let cool completely in the dish on a wire rack

To assemble the cake, spread the frosting over the top of the cake. Sprinkle the wafer crumbs over the frosting so they look like dirt. Decorate the top with the gummy worms. Serve right away, or to store, cover tightly with plastic wrap and refrigerate for up to 2 days.

Recipe Note
To make 2 cups chocolate crumbs, in a food processor, process 10 ounces chocolate wafers or chocolate graham crackers until finely ground.

Tres Leches Cake

This cake gets its name from the three types of milk—*tres leches*—used in the sauce that give it an extraordinary texture: sweetened condensed milk, evaporated milk, and heavy cream. Feel free to omit the rum in the sauce and replace it with an extra teaspoon of vanilla extract.

MAKES 10–12 SERVINGS

FOR THE CAKE

½ cup vegetable shortening, plus more for the pan

2¼ cups sifted all-purpose flour, plus more for the pan

2 teaspoons baking powder

½ teaspoon salt

1 cup whole milk

1 teaspoon vanilla extract

1½ cups sugar

2 large eggs

FOR THE SAUCE

1 can (14 ounces) sweetened condensed milk

1 can (12 fluid ounces) evaporated milk

½ cup heavy cream

3 tablespoons dark rum

1 teaspoon vanilla extract

Preheat the oven to 350°F. Grease the bottom and sides of a 9-by-13-inch baking pan with shortening, then dust with flour, tapping out the excess.

To make the cake, in a medium bowl, sift together the flour, baking powder, and salt. In a small bowl, whisk together the milk and vanilla. In a large bowl, using an electric mixer, beat the shortening on high speed until fluffy, about 2 minutes. Add the sugar a little at a time, beating after each addition until fluffy. On low speed, add the eggs one at a time, beating after each addition until incorporated. Add one-third of the milk mixture to the egg-shortening mixture and beat on low speed until well mixed. Then add one-third of the flour mixture and beat until well mixed. Repeat twice more with the remaining milk mixture and flour mixture, beating well after each addition. Scrape the batter into the prepared pan and spread evenly.

Bake the cake until a toothpick inserted into the center comes out clean, about 35 minutes. Let cool in the pan on a wire rack for 10 minutes, then invert the cake onto a platter, lift off the pan, and let cool completely.

To make the sauce, in a medium bowl, whisk together the condensed milk, evaporated milk, cream, rum, and vanilla, mixing well. Poke the top of the cooled cake all over with a fork, then spoon the sauce evenly over the surface a little at a time, allowing the cake to absorb the sauce before adding more. A little sauce may pool on the platter. Cover the cake with plastic wrap and refrigerate for about 1 hour.

FOR THE MERINGUE FROSTING

¾ cup sugar

½ cup water

3 large egg whites

¼ teaspoon cream of tartar

To make the frosting, first make a caramel syrup. In a medium saucepan, combine the sugar and water and stir to moisten the sugar evenly. Place over medium-high heat and bring to a boil, stirring to dissolve the sugar. Reduce the heat to a simmer and cook, without stirring, until the caramel syrup registers 230°F on a candy thermometer, 10–12 minutes. If sugar crystals form on the sides of the pan, wash them down with a pastry brush dipped in cold water. While the caramel is cooking, in a large bowl, using the electric mixer, beat together the egg whites and cream of tartar on medium speed until foamy. Increase the speed to high and beat until stiff peaks form. When the caramel syrup is ready, with the mixer on high speed, slowly add the hot syrup in a thin stream to the beaten egg whites, aiming it away from the beater and close to the side of the bowl, until all the syrup is incorporated. Continue beating the frosting until it is cooled and glossy.

Spread the frosting over the top of the cake. Cover with plastic wrap (use toothpicks to tent the plastic wrap away from the frosted surface) and refrigerate until well chilled, at least 3 hours or for up to 8 hours. Serve chilled.

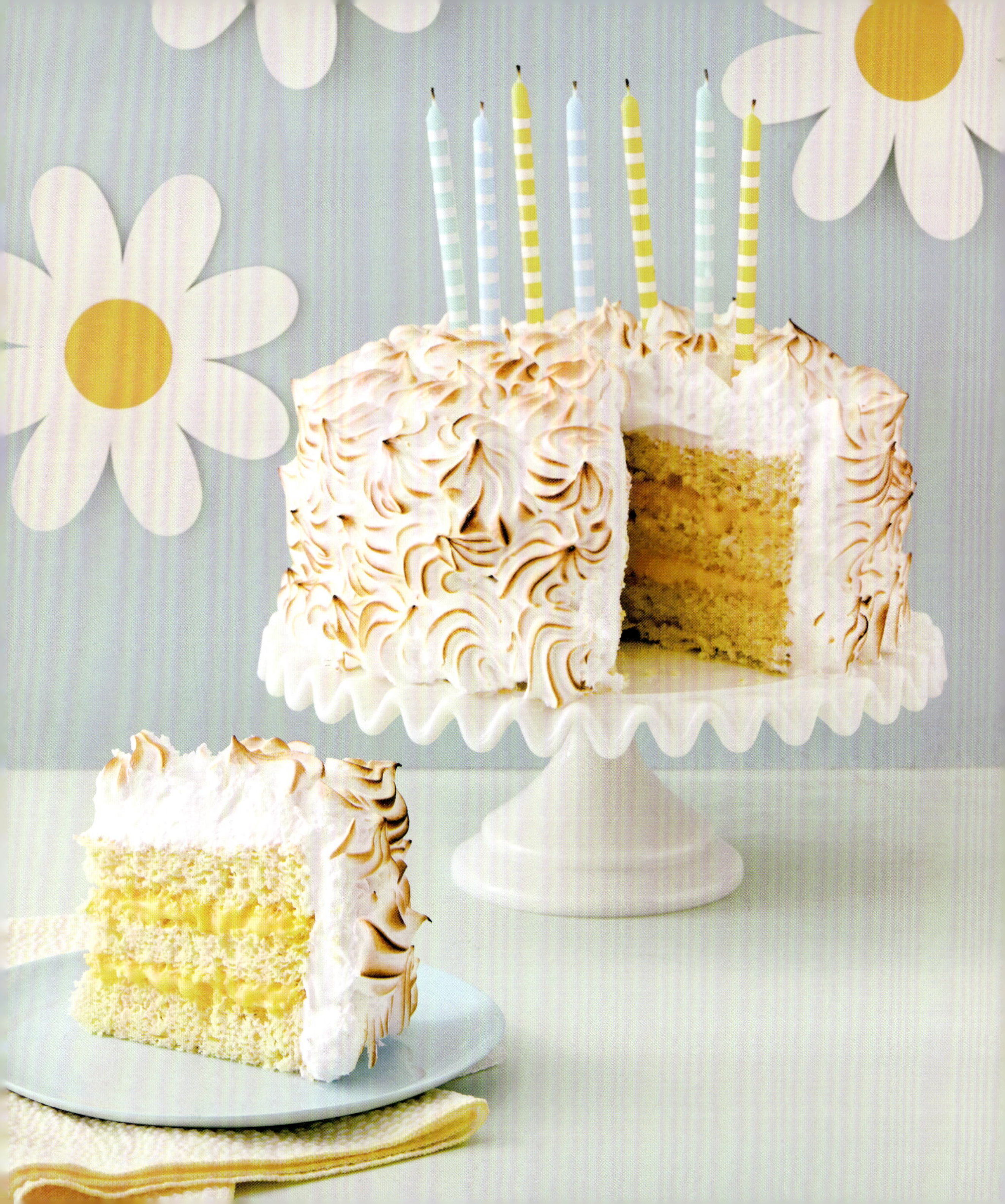

Lemon Meringue Layer Cake

The cake used in this riff on a lemon meringue pie is a classic genoise, heavy on the eggs and light on the flour. It's a great all-purpose cake that can be used with any of the frostings in this book. For a vanilla version, omit the lemon zest and add 2 teaspoons vanilla bean paste to the batter.

MAKES 10–12 SERVINGS

Lemon Curd (page 145)

½ cup all-purpose flour

½ cup cornstarch

9 large eggs, separated, plus 1 large whole egg

1 cup sugar

1 tablespoon finely grated lemon zest

¾ cup (1½ sticks) unsalted butter, melted and cooled

Meringue Frosting (page 139)

Make the lemon curd and refrigerate as directed.

Preheat the oven to 325°F (165°C). Line the bottoms of three 8-inch round cake pans with parchment paper.

In a medium bowl, sift together the flour and cornstarch. In a second medium bowl, using an electric mixer, beat together the egg yolks and the whole egg on medium speed until blended. Increase the speed to medium-high and slowly add ½ cup of the sugar, then continue to beat until the mixture is pale and has tripled in volume, 3–5 minutes. Set aside.

In a large bowl, using the electric mixer with clean beaters, beat the egg whites on medium speed until foamy. Increase the speed to medium-high, slowly add the remaining ½ cup sugar, and beat until stiff peaks form, 3–5 minutes.

Using a rubber spatula, gently fold the egg yolk mixture into the egg white mixture just until incorporated. Sift the flour mixture over the egg mixture, scatter the lemon zest on top, and fold in until the flour streaks begin to disappear. Then add the melted butter and fold in just until incorporated and no white streaks are visible.

Continued on page 42

Lemon Lover

Serve sparkling lemonade with this bright citrusy cake. Carry over the yellow color into the party decor, with paper daisy cutouts and cheery napkins.

~ *Continued from page 41* ~

Divide the batter evenly among the prepared cake pans and spread evenly. Bake the cake layers until they spring back when lightly touched and a toothpick inserted into the center comes out with just a few moist crumbs attached, about 30 minutes. Let cool in the pans on wire racks for 10 minutes, then invert the cakes onto the racks, lift off the pans, peel off the parchment, and let cool completely.

To assemble the cake, place a cake layer on a serving plate. Spread half of the lemon curd over the top. Place a second layer on top and spread the remaining curd over the cake. Top with the third layer and refrigerate while you prepare the frosting.

Spoon the frosting into a large piping bag fitted with an open star tip, being careful not to deflate the frosting. Starting at the base of the cake, pipe florets around and up the sides, finishing on the top. Using a kitchen torch, toast the meringue until nicely browned. Serve right away.

Eight-Layer Honey Pistachio Cake

You don't need eight cake pans to make this impressive cake. The layers are giant honey graham cracker cookies, which are baked on a sheet pan and then sandwiched with vanilla-scented sour cream frosting. Be sure to make this cake a day ahead so the crisp, graham cracker–like cake layers soften.

MAKES 10–12 SERVINGS

FOR THE CAKE

3 cups all-purpose flour, plus more for the work surface

1 teaspoon baking soda

½ teaspoon salt

½ cup honey

½ cup granulated sugar

2 tablespoons unsalted butter

3 large eggs

FOR THE FROSTING

1 cup heavy cream

4 cups sour cream

2 cups powdered sugar

1 teaspoon vanilla extract

¼ teaspoon salt

½ cup pistachio nuts, toasted and crushed

Preheat the oven to 350°F. Line the bottom of a rimmed baking sheet with parchment paper.

To make the cake, in a medium bowl, sift together the flour, baking soda, and salt. In a large saucepan over medium heat, combine the honey, granulated sugar, and butter and cook, stirring occasionally, until the butter melts and the sugar and honey dissolve, about 5 minutes. Remove from the heat and let cool slightly.

In a small bowl, whisk the eggs until blended. Add a few tablespoons of the warm honey mixture to the eggs and whisk until blended. While whisking constantly, gradually add the egg mixture to the honey mixture in the saucepan. Using a rubber spatula, fold the flour mixture into the honey-egg mixture until almost incorporated and a cookie-like dough forms. Transfer the dough to a lightly floured work surface and knead just enough to form a thick disk. Divide the disk into 8 equal pieces. Cover the pieces with a kitchen towel to prevent them from drying out.

On the lightly floured surface, roll out a piece of dough into a 9-inch round. Place an 8-inch plate or cake pan as a template on the center of the round and, using a small, sharp knife, cut around the edge of the template to create an 8-inch dough round. Set the scraps aside. Repeat with a second dough piece. Transfer the 2 rounds to the prepared baking sheet and bake until crisp and golden brown, about 6 minutes. Transfer the rounds to wire racks and let cool completely.

~ Continued on page 44 ~

~ *Continued from page 43* ~

While the first 2 rounds are baking, roll and cut out 2 more rounds, then bake and cool the same way. Repeat until you have baked a total of 8 rounds. When they cool, they should have the texture of graham crackers. Spread the reserved dough scraps in a single layer on the baking sheet and bake until crisp and golden brown, about 6 minutes. Let cool completely on the pan on a wire rack.

To make the frosting, in a bowl, using an electric mixer, beat the heavy cream on medium-high speed until stiff peaks form, about 3 minutes. In a large bowl, whisk together the sour cream, powdered sugar, vanilla, and salt. Using a rubber spatula, gently fold the whipped cream into the sour cream mixture just until evenly incorporated.

To assemble the cake, line a rimmed baking sheet with parchment paper or use a cardboard cake circle. Place a cake round on the prepared pan or cake circle. Spread about ½ cup of the sour cream frosting evenly over the cake round, extending it to the edges (it's okay if a little spills over the edge). Top with a second cake round and spread with frosting. Repeat with the remaining cake rounds, spreading each one with frosting. When the final cake round is in place, spread the remaining frosting evenly over the top and sides of the cake. Put the baked dough scraps into a heavy plastic bag and crush with a rolling pin. Press the crumbs evenly onto the sides of the cake. Sprinkle the pistachios over the top.

Cover the cake with a cake dome or with plastic wrap (use toothpicks to tent the plastic wrap away from the frosted surface) and refrigerate overnight. The frosting will soften the layers into a cakelike texture. Serve chilled or at room temperature.

Berries and Cream Roulade

A roulade, or rolled cake, is an impressive birthday dessert and can be a bit daunting to make. But with a little patience and practice, you can perfect this three-ingredient cake. Choose the sweetest fresh berries you can find for the filling and be sure not to overwhip the crème fraîche–scented cream.

MAKES 8–10 SERVINGS

FOR THE CAKE

Unsalted butter, at room temperature, for the pan

4 large eggs

⅓ cup plus 1 tablespoon granulated sugar

1 cup cake flour

FOR THE FILLING AND TOPPING

1¾ cups cold heavy cream

¾ cup crème fraîche

1 cup mixed berries, such as whole raspberries, blackberries, or blueberries or sliced strawberries, in any combination, plus 15 whole berries or berry slices for garnish

1 tablespoon powdered sugar

To make the cake, preheat the oven to 475°F. Butter an 18-by-13-inch baking sheet with 1-inch sides. Line the bottom with parchment paper.

Separate 2 of the eggs, dropping the yolks into a large bowl and the whites into a medium bowl. Crack the remaining 2 whole eggs into the bowl with the yolks. Using an electric mixer, beat the egg yolks and whole eggs on medium speed while slowly adding the ⅓ cup granulated sugar in a steady stream. Increase the speed to high and beat until the mixture has almost doubled in volume, about 5 minutes.

Using clean beaters, beat the egg whites on medium speed until they start to foam. Slowly add the remaining 1 tablespoon granulated sugar while continuing to beat on medium speed. Increase the speed to high and beat until the whites form soft peaks but still look wet. Using a rubber spatula, gently fold the whites into the egg yolk mixture. Sift the flour over the combined egg mixtures and gently fold in with a rubber spatula just until incorporated. Pour the batter into the prepared pan and spread evenly.

~ Continued on page 46 ~

> **Party It Up!**
> Show off this special rolled cake on a colorful platter garnished with fresh berries. You can also dust the top with cocoa powder, or drizzle chocolate sauce on each slice.

~ *Continued from page 45* ~

Bake the cake, rotating the pan back to front halfway through, until springy to the touch, 5–8 minutes. Remove from the oven and slide a table knife around the inside edge of the pan to loosen the cake sides. Then slip the knife under one end of the cake, lift slightly, and slide the cake, still on the parchment, onto a wire rack. Starting from a long side, gently roll up the cake with the parchment into a log (this will "train" it to not crack when you fill the roulade). Let cool completely.

To make the filling, in a medium bowl, using the electric mixer, beat together ¾ cup of the cream and the crème fraîche on medium speed until soft peaks form. Using the rubber spatula, gently fold in the 1 cup berries.

Lay a sheet of parchment paper slightly larger than the flat cake on a work surface. Unroll the cooled cake with its parchment, cake side down, onto the parchment sheet, then peel off the original parchment. Spread the cream-berry mixture evenly over the cake. Working from the long side nearest you, roll up the cake, working carefully to keep the roll even, into a log. Transfer, seam side down, to a serving plate.

To make the topping, in a medium bowl, using the electric mixer, beat together the remaining 1 cup cream and the powdered sugar on medium speed until soft peaks form. Spoon the whipped cream into a piping bag fitted with a ¾-inch open star tip and pipe a spiral down the center of the cake. Set the whole berries in the curves of the spiral for garnish. Cover and refrigerate until ready to serve.

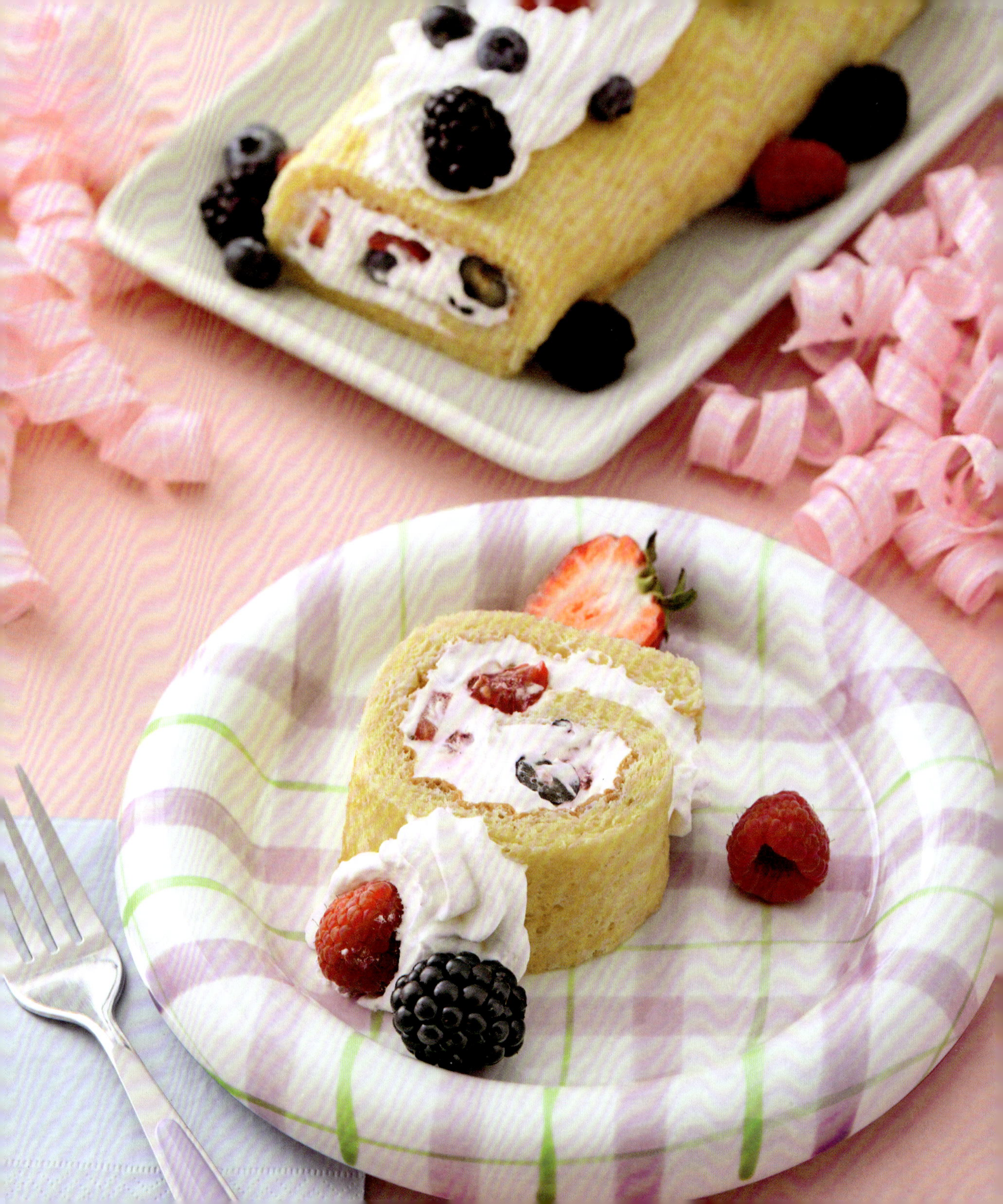

Vanilla Bean Cheesecake with Fresh Fruit

A lofty cheesecake piled high with fresh berries, nectarines, or plums is a fruit lover's birthday dream. Be sure to plan ahead because the cake must be made a day in advance of serving to allow time for it to set properly.

MAKES 10–12 SERVINGS

FOR THE CRUST

4 tablespoons (½ stick) unsalted butter, melted, plus more at room temperature for the pan

½ cup slivered almonds, toasted

8 whole honey graham crackers (about 4 ounces)

2 tablespoons sugar

¼ teaspoon salt

Preheat the oven to 350°F. Butter the bottom and sides of a 9-inch springform pan.

To make the crust, in a food processor, pulse the almonds until finely ground. Add the graham crackers and process to fine crumbs. Add the melted butter, sugar, and salt and process until well mixed and the crumbs are evenly moistened.

Transfer the crumb mixture to the prepared pan and, using your fingertips, press the mixture evenly onto the bottom and about 1 inch up the sides of the pan. Bake until fragrant and toasted, about 10 minutes. Let cool completely on a wire rack.

Reduce the oven temperature to 325°F.

To make the filling, wipe the processor bowl clean, then add the cream cheese and process until creamy. Add the sugar and process until smooth. Stop the processor and scrape down the bowl with a rubber spatula. Add the eggs one at a time, processing after each addition until incorporated. Stop the processor and scrape down the bowl again. Using the tip of a kinfe, scrape out the seeds from inside the vanilla bean. Add to the cream cheese mixture along with the lemon juice and vanilla extract and process until smooth and creamy.

Place the crust on a rimmed baking sheet and pour the batter into the crust. Cover the springform pan with a large pot lid or another baking sheet to insulate the cheesecake while it bakes. Bake the cheesecake until the center

FOR THE FILLING

2 pounds cream cheese, at room temperature

1 cup sugar

3 large eggs, at room temperature

1 vanilla bean, split lengthwise

2 tablespoons fresh lemon juice

1 tablespoon vanilla extract

FOR THE TOPPING

2 cups sour cream

¼ cup sugar

1 vanilla bean, split lengthwise, or 2 teaspoons vanilla extract

About 3 cups ripe fresh fruit, such as sliced strawberries, nectarines, or plums or mixed berries

jiggles very slightly when the pan is gently shaken, 45–50 minutes. If the center looks soupy, re-cover the cheesecake and continue to bake for a few more minutes.

Meanwhile, make the topping. In a small bowl, stir together sour cream and sugar until the sugar dissolves. Scrape the seeds from the vanilla bean and add to the bowl or add the vanilla extract. Stir until all the ingredients are well mixed. Cover and set aside at room temperature until needed.

Remove the cheesecake from the oven and uncover it. Carefully pour the topping around the edge of the cheesecake, then, using an offset spatula, gently spread the topping evenly over the entire surface. Do not press too hard, or the topping will sink into the cake.

Re-cover the cheesecake, return it to the oven, and bake for another 5 minutes to set the topping. Transfer the cheesecake to a rack and let cool completely, covered, for 1–2 hours. Remove the baking sheet or pot lid, cover the pan with a large flat plate, and refrigerate the cheesecake overnight.

To unmold the cheesecake, release the pan sides, opening them widely so they fall away from the cake. Loosen the bottom crust from the pan base with a thin, flat butter knife or offset spatula and slide the cake off the base onto a serving plate.

Serve the cheesecake chilled, topped with the fruit. To store the cake, put it into an airtight container and refrigerate for up to 5 days.

Cupcakes

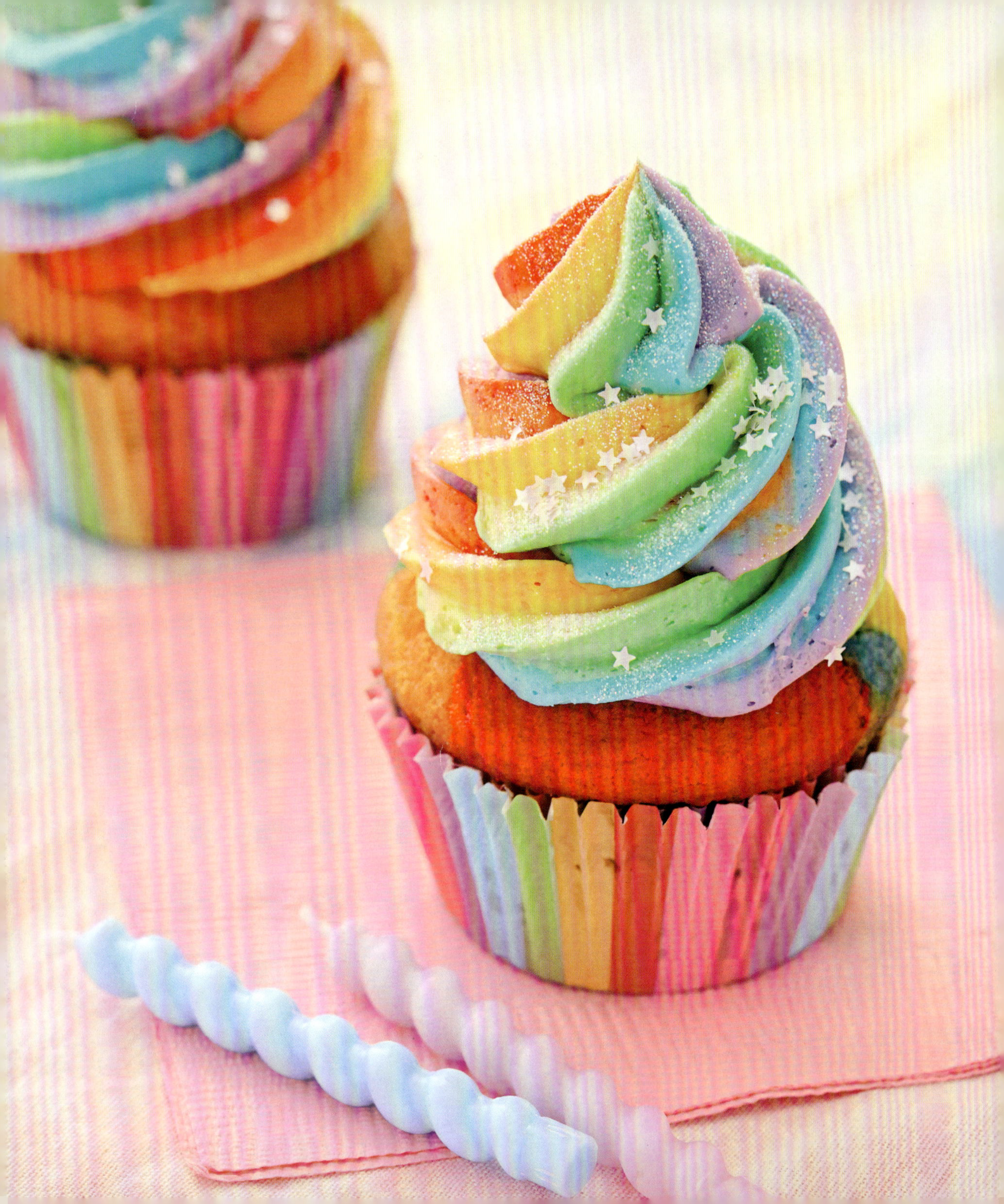

Rainbow Glitter Cupcakes

An explosion of rainbow colors—in both the cake and the frosting—these cupcakes are the perfect choice for every sparkly birthday person. But the color doesn't stop there. They are topped with sparkling sugar, rainbow sprinkles, or edible glitter. You can also kick it up a notch and finish them with a mixture of all three!

MAKES 12 CUPCAKES

1½ cups all-purpose flour

1½ teaspoons baking powder

½ teaspoon baking soda

¼ teaspoon salt

½ cup (1 stick) unsalted butter, at cool room temperature

¾ cup granulated sugar

2 large eggs

1 teaspoon vanilla extract

½ cup sour cream or plain whole-milk yogurt

Red, orange, yellow, green, blue, and purple gel food coloring

Vanilla Frosting (page 136)

Sparkling sugar, rainbow sprinkles, and/or edible glitter, for decorating

Preheat the oven to 350°F. Line 12 standard muffins cups with paper liners.

In a medium bowl, whisk together the flour, baking powder, baking soda, and salt. In a large bowl, using an electric mixer, beat together the butter and granulated sugar on medium-high speed until pale and fluffy, about 3 minutes. Beat in the eggs one at a time, beating after each addition until incorporated. Add the vanilla and beat until blended. Stop the mixer and scrape down the bowl with a rubber spatula. On low speed, add half of the flour mixture and beat just until blended, then add the sour cream and beat just until mixed. Add the remaining flour and beat just until blended. Stop the mixer and scrape down the bowl. Beat one last time on medium speed until well blended, about 10 seconds.

Divide the batter evenly among 6 small bowls. Add a few drops of a different color of food coloring—red, orange, yellow, green, blue, and purple—to each bowl, stirring it into the batter. You will have 6 different colors of the rainbow. Dollop a heaping teaspoonful of each color into each prepared muffin cup. Make sure each color is evenly distributed among the 12 cups.

Continued on page 54

> **Over-the-Rainbow Fun**
> Pair these cupcakes with a rainbow-themed celebration: decorate with matching streamers and plates, and don't forget a pot of gold that's full of goodies to share.

~ *Continued from page 53* ~

Bake the cupcakes until a toothpick inserted into the center of a cupcake comes out clean, 15–18 minutes. Let cool in the pan on a wire rack for 15 minutes, then carefully transfer the cupcakes directly to the rack and let cool completely, about 1¼ hours.

Lay a large piece of plastic wrap—about 12 by 16 inches—on a clean work surface. Spoon each colored frosting into a separate lock-top plastic bag, twist the top closed, and cut off a corner. Beginning at a narrow end of the plastic wrap, pipe thick 11-inch-long vertical stripes of each frosting color side by side in rainbow order (red, orange, yellow, green, blue, purple), starting 1 inch in from a long edge of the plastic wrap and finishing at the middle of the plastic wrap. Repeat the rainbow stripes, leaving a 1-inch border at the opposite edge, so you have two rows of each color. Fold the 1-inch border over the frosting, then roll up the plastic wrap like a jelly roll. Twist one end closed and leave the other end open.

Fit a large piping bag with a medium-large star tip and insert the frosting roll, open end first, into the bag. Push the frosting down toward the tip and twist the top of the bag closed. Pipe a rainbow swirl of frosting onto each cupcake. Decorate each cupcake with sparkling sugar.

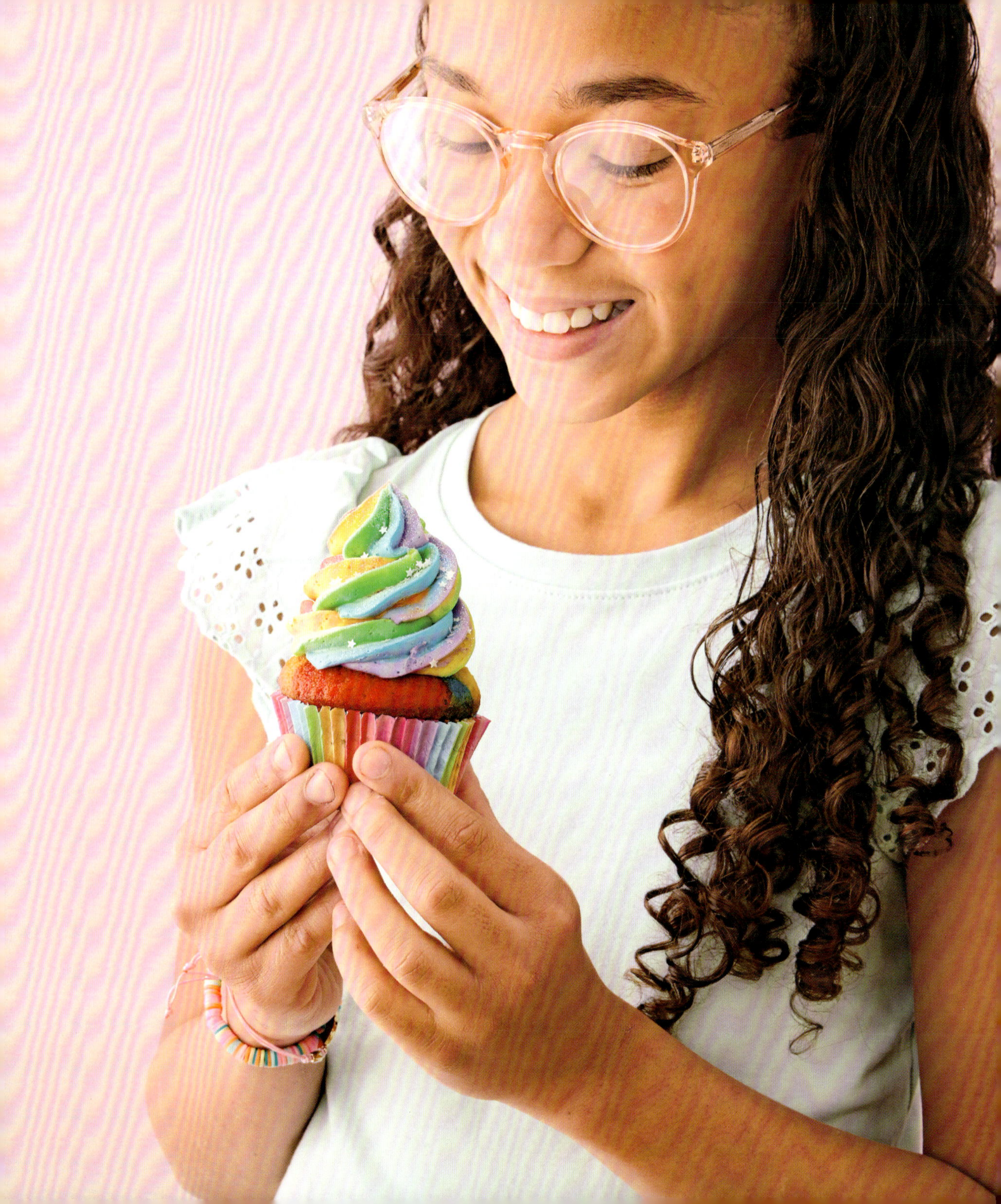

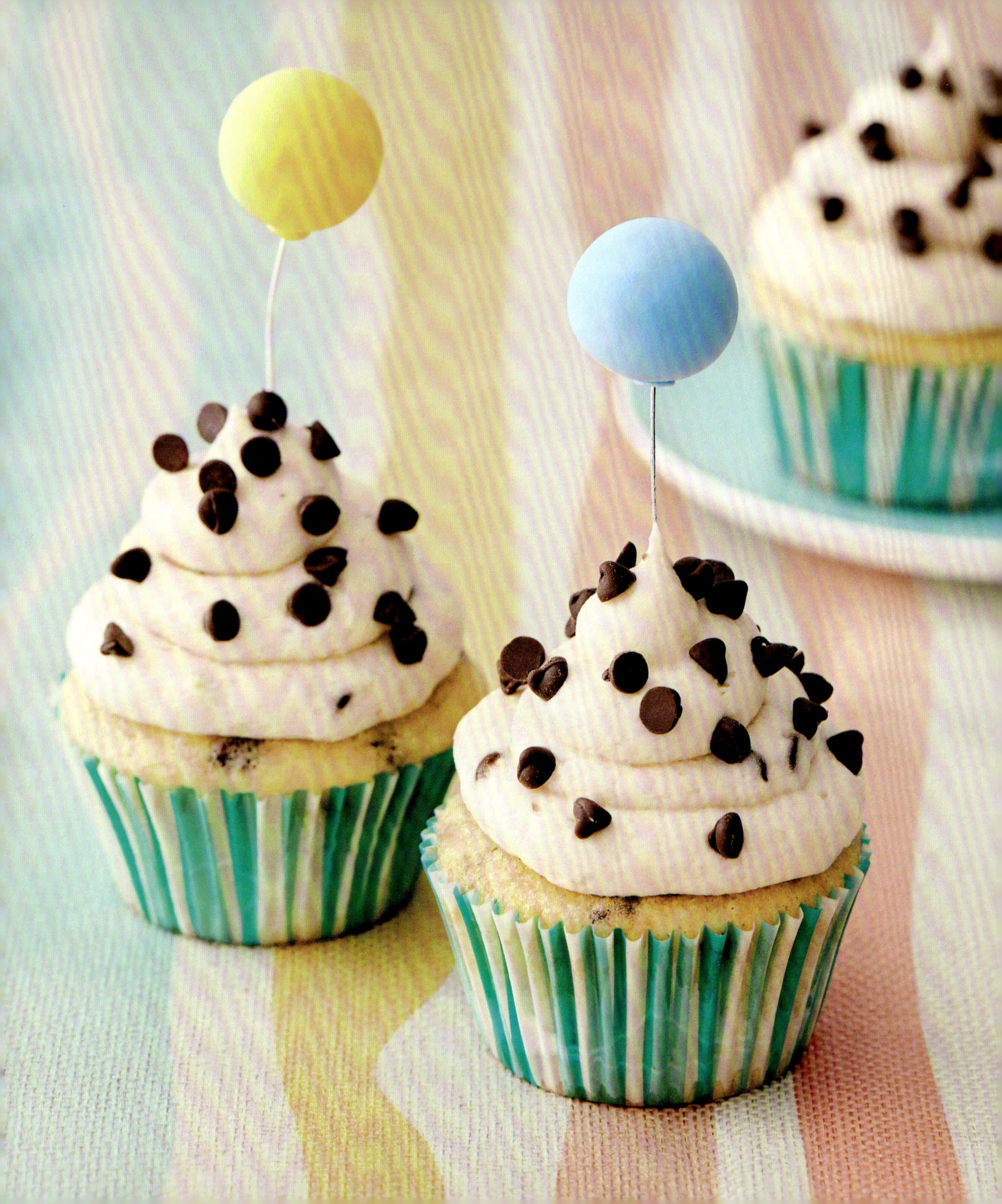

Chocolate Chip Cookie Dough Cupcakes

As if chocolate chip cupcakes aren't enough, each cupcake conceals a delicious scoop of chocolate chip cookie dough, and, for double happiness, some of the dough is also whipped into the frosting. Heat treating the flour for the edible cookie dough makes it safe for eating, so don't skip this step.

MAKES 12 CUPCAKES

FOR THE EDIBLE COOKIE DOUGH

¾ cup all-purpose flour

6 tablespoons (¾ stick) unsalted butter, at cool room temperature

½ cup firmly packed light brown sugar

2 tablespoons whole milk

1 teaspoon vanilla extract

¼ teaspoon salt

½ cup mini chocolate chips

To make the cookie dough, in a small microwave-safe bowl, microwave the flour on high power for 1½ minutes, stopping to stir every 30 seconds. In a medium bowl, using an electric mixer, beat together the butter and brown sugar on medium-high speed until creamy, about 1 minute. Add the milk, vanilla, and salt and beat until blended. Sift the flour over the butter mixture and beat on low speed until mixed, then beat in the chocolate chips.

Line a small rimmed baking sheet with parchment paper. Scoop up 12 tablespoon-size portions of the dough. Roll each portion into a ball between your palms and arrange on the prepared pan. Cover and refrigerate the dough balls while you make the cupcakes. You should have about ⅓ cup dough remaining, which you will add to the frosting. Transfer it to an airtight container and set aside at room temperature.

To make the cupcakes, preheat the oven to 350°F. Line 12 standard muffin cups with paper or foil liners.

In a medium bowl, whisk together the flour, baking powder, and salt. In a large bowl, using the electric mixer, beat together the butter and granulated sugar on medium-high speed until pale and fluffy, 2–3 minutes. Add the eggs one at a time, beating after each addition until incorporated. Add the vanilla and beat until blended. Stop the mixer and scrape down the bowl with a rubber spatula. On low speed, add about half of the flour mixture and beat just until blended.

Continued on page 58

~ Continued from page 57 ~

FOR THE CUPCAKES

1¼ cups all-purpose flour

1½ teaspoons baking powder

¼ teaspoon salt

6 tablespoons unsalted butter, at cool room temperature

¾ cup granulated sugar

2 large eggs

1 teaspoon vanilla extract

⅓ cup whole milk

½ cup mini chocolate chips

Cookie Dough Frosting (page 136)

2 tablespoons mini chocolate chips, for decorating (optional)

Add the milk and beat until incorporated, then add the remaining flour mixture and beat just until blended. Stop the mixer, scrape down the bowl, and give the batter a final stir with the spatula.

Divide the batter evenly among the prepared muffin cups, filling them about three-fourths full. Bake until the tops are light golden brown and a toothpick inserted into the center of a cupcake comes out clean, 18–20 minutes. Let cool in the pan on a wire rack for 10 minutes, then carefully transfer the cupcakes directly to the rack. Using a paring knife, cut out a round from the top of each cupcake just large enough to hold a cookie dough ball, then place a dough ball in the center of each cupcake. Let cool completely, about 1 hour. (Enjoy the nuggets of removed cupcake as a baker's treat.)

Make the frosting as directed, adding the reserved cookie dough to it. Using a small offset spatula or a piping bag fitted with a large round tip, top the cupcakes with the frosting. Decorate the frosting with the chocolate chips, if you like.

Fun Toppers

Dress up your cupcakes with party-themed or colorful toppers. Look online for festive mini pom-poms, flags, flowers, balloons, tiaras, stars, butterflies, and more.

Cookies and Cream Cupcakes

If cookies and cream is your favorite ice cream flavor, these cupcakes are for you! Here, moist cocoa cupcakes are topped with creamy-dreamy Cookies and Cream Frosting and finished with a whole chocolate sandwich cookie.

MAKES 18 CUPCAKES

1 cup boiling water

¾ cup unsweetened natural cocoa powder

1¾ cups all-purpose flour

1½ teaspoons baking soda

¼ teaspoon salt

1½ cups sugar

4 tablespoons (½ stick) unsalted butter, at cool room temperature

3 large eggs

1 teaspoon vanilla extract

1¼ cups buttermilk

Cookies and Cream Frosting (page 136)

18 chocolate sandwich cookies, for garnish

Preheat the oven to 350°F. Line 18 standard muffin cups with paper liners.

In a small heatproof bowl, whisk together the boiling water and cocoa powder until smooth. Let cool completely.

In a bowl, sift together the flour, baking soda, and salt. In a large bowl, using an electric mixer, beat together the sugar and butter on medium-high speed until pale and fluffy, about 3 minutes. Beat in the eggs one at a time, beating after each addition until incorporated. Add the vanilla and the cooled cocoa mixture and beat until blended. On low speed, add the flour mixture in three additions alternately with the buttermilk in two additions, beginning and ending with the flour mixture and beating just until blended after each addition. As you work, stop the mixer to scrape down the bowl with a rubber spatula as needed.

Divide the batter evenly among the prepared cups, filling them about three-fourths full. Bake until the tops spring back when pressed in the center, 20–25 minutes. Carefully transfer the cupcakes to wire racks and let cool completely, about 1 hour.

Spoon the frosting into a piping bag fitted with a large open star tip and pipe decoratively onto the cupcakes. Top each cupcake with a sandwich cookie.

Ice Cream Cone Cupcakes

Baked in ice cream cones, these memorable cupcakes are topped with piped Vanilla Frosting dipped in chocolate glaze to mimic soft-serve ice cream.

MAKES 12 CUPCAKES

12 jumbo flat-bottomed wafer ice cream cones

1¼ cups all-purpose flour

1¼ teaspoons baking powder

¼ teaspoon salt

¾ cup sugar

6 tablespoons (¾ stick) unsalted butter, at room temperature

2 large eggs

1 teaspoon vanilla extract

⅓ cup whole milk

Vanilla Frosting (page 136)

Chocolate Glaze (page 144), warmed slightly

½ cup rainbow sprinkles

12 maraschino cherries

Preheat the oven to 350°F. Stand an ice cream cone in each cup of a 12-cup standard muffin pan (or use two 6-cup muffin pans).

In a medium bowl, whisk together the flour, baking powder, and salt. In a large bowl, using an electric mixer, beat together the sugar and butter on medium-high speed until pale and fluffy, 2–3 minutes. Add the eggs one at a time, beating after each addition until incorporated. Stop the mixer and scrape down the bowl with a rubber spatula. Add the vanilla and beat on medium-high speed until combined. On low speed, add about half of the flour mixture and beat just until blended. Add the milk and beat just until mixed, then add the remaining flour mixture and beat just until blended. Stop the mixer, scrape down the bowl, and give the batter a final stir with the rubber spatula.

Divide the batter evenly among the cones, filling each one about two-thirds full. Bake the cupcakes until the tops are light golden brown and a toothpick inserted into the center comes out clean, 18–20 minutes. Let cool in the pan on a wire rack for 10 minutes, then carefully transfer directly to the rack and let cool completely.

Spoon two-thirds of the frosting into a piping bag fitted with a large round tip and pipe a thick, even layer onto each cupcake, starting from the outer edge and spiraling toward the center. Return the cupcakes to the muffin pan and freeze for 20 minutes to firm up the frosting.

Put the glaze and the sprinkles in separate bowls. Dip the frosted part of each cupcake first into the glaze and then into the sprinkles. Return to the pan and freeze for 5 minutes. Using the remaining frosting and an open star tip, pipe a swirl onto each cupcake and top with a cherry.

Special Service

To dress up these cuties, tie a wide ribbon around the base of each cone before serving and add a tag with each guest's name. You can trade out the sprinkles for chopped peanuts.

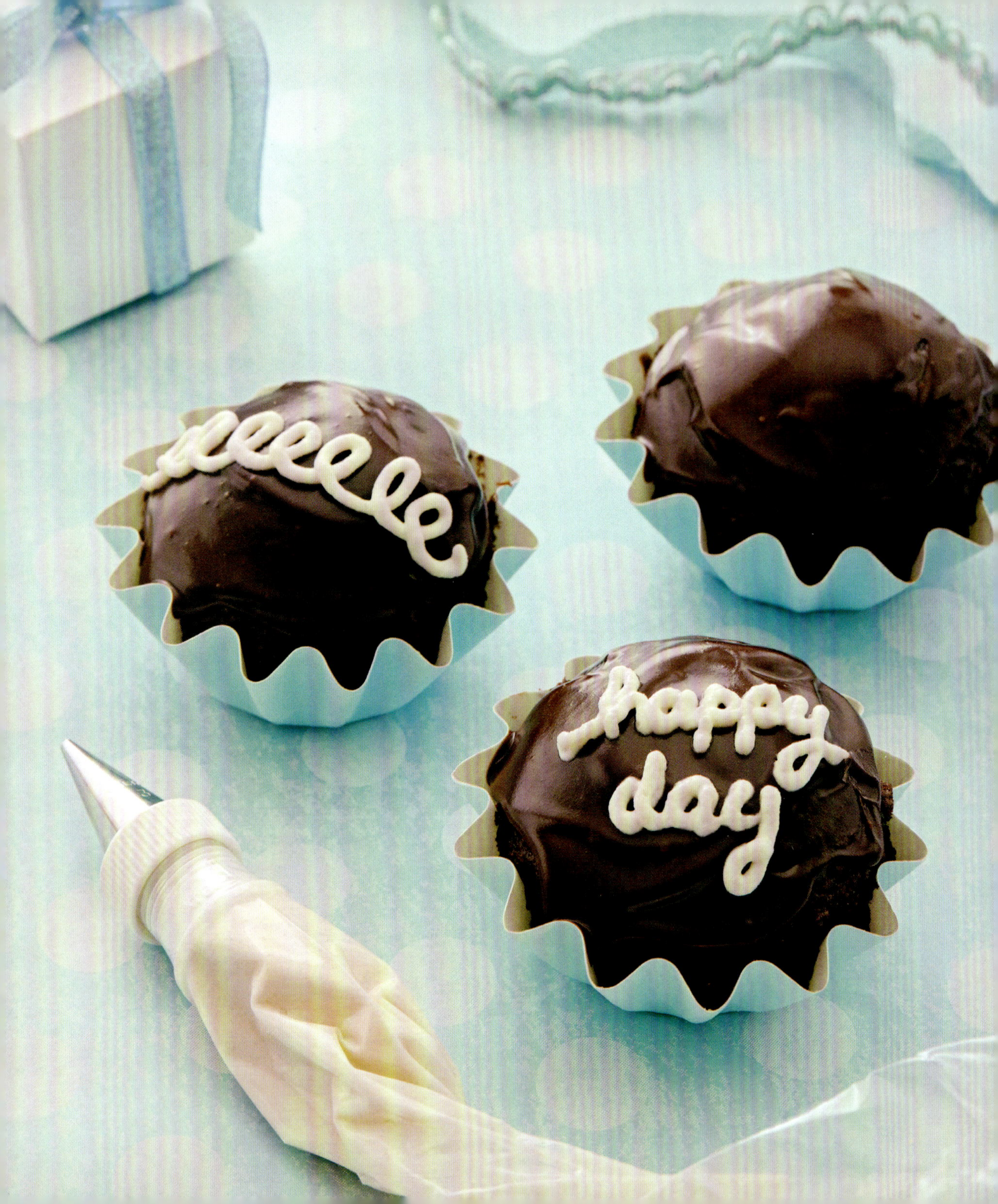
happy day

Choco-Mallow Cupcakes

The base of these cupcakes is rich devil's food, which is filled with a scoop of fluffy marshmallow cream. Chocolate glaze caps them off, and for a real treat (and a nostalgic nod to the classic cream-filled, foil-wrapped chocolate cakelets), pipe a swirl of vanilla frosting across the top.

MAKES 18 CUPCAKES

Devil's Food Cupcakes (page 64), batter only

FOR THE FILLING

¾ cup powdered sugar

3 tablespoons unsalted butter, at room temperature

½ cup marshmallow creme

1 tablespoon heavy cream

½ teaspoon vanilla extract

Chocolate Glaze (page 144)

¼ cup Vanilla Frosting (page 136)

Preheat the oven to 350°F. Line 18 standard muffin cups with paper liners.

Make the cupcake batter as directed. Divide the batter evenly among the prepared muffin cups, filling each one about three-fourths full. Bake until a toothpick inserted into the center of a cupcake comes out clean, 20–25 minutes. Carefully remove the cupcakes from the pans and let cool completely on wire racks, about 30 minutes.

To make the filling, in a medium bowl, using an electric mixer, beat together the sugar and butter on medium speed until lightened, about 3 minutes. Stop the mixer and scrape down the bowl with a rubber spatula. Add the marshmallow creme, heavy cream, and vanilla and beat on medium speed until light and fluffy, about 3 minutes.

To fill the cupcakes, using a paring knife, cut a round about 1½ inches in diameter and about 1 inch deep in the center of each cupcake and remove the rounds (enjoy them as a baker's treat). Fill each hollow with a spoonful of the filling.

Spoon the glaze over the filled cupcakes. Let stand until mostly set, about 30 minutes. Spoon the frosting into a small piping bag fitted with a small round tip and pipe a swirl (or write something cute) on the top of each cupcake. Let set for 30 minutes before serving.

Devil's Food Cupcakes

Legend has it that devil's food gets its name not because it is evil but because it is sinfully good. Its deep, dark color is the result of adding extra baking soda, which neutralizes the acid in the cocoa powder, turning the cocoa darker. If you like a lot of frosting, double the recipe.

MAKES 18 CUPCAKES

1 cup boiling water

¾ cup unsweetened natural cocoa powder

1¾ cups all-purpose flour

1½ teaspoons baking soda

¼ teaspoon salt

1½ cups sugar

4 tablespoons (½ stick) unsalted butter, at cool room temperature

3 large eggs

1 teaspoon vanilla extract

1¼ cups buttermilk

Dark Chocolate Frosting (page 143)

Sprinkles, for decorating (optional)

Preheat the oven to 350°F. Line 18 standard muffin cups with paper liners.

In a small heatproof bowl, whisk together the boiling water and cocoa powder until smooth. Let cool completely.

In a medium bowl, sift together the flour, baking soda, and salt. In a large bowl, using an electric mixer, beat together the sugar and butter on medium-high speed until pale and fluffy, about 3 minutes. Beat in the eggs one at a time, beating after each addition until incorporated. Add the vanilla and the cooled cocoa mixture and beat until well mixed. On low speed, add the flour mixture in three additions alternately with the buttermilk in two additions, beginning and ending with the flour mixture and beating after each addition just until blended. As you work, stop the mixer and scrape down the bowl with a rubber spatula as needed.

Divide the batter evenly among the prepared cups, filling each one about three-fourths full. Bake until the tops spring back when pressed in the center, 20–25 minutes. Carefully remove the cupcakes from the pans and let cool completely on wire racks, about 30 minutes.

Spoon the frosting into a piping bag fitted with a large star tip and pipe decoratively onto the cupcakes. Decorate with sprinkles, if you like.

Mini Mint-Chocolate Chip Cupcakes

What is cuter than a mini cupcake? A mini minty chocolate chip–laced chocolate cupcake with green Mint Frosting. Decorate these cuties with your favorite chocolate mint candies and fresh mint leaves and serve them on a tiered stand.

MAKES 24 MINI CUPCAKES

4 ounces bittersweet chocolate, chopped

4 tablespoons (½ stick) unsalted butter, cut into chunks

¾ cup sugar

2 large eggs

½ teaspoon vanilla extract

¼ teaspoon peppermint extract

¼ teaspoon salt

¼ cup plus 2 tablespoons all-purpose flour

½ cup mini chocolate chips

Mint Frosting (page 136)

Soft chocolate mint candies, such as Junior Mints, for decorating (optional)

Small fresh mint leaves, for decorating (optional)

Preheat the oven to 350°F. Line 24 mini muffin cups with paper or foil liners.

In a medium microwave-safe bowl, combine the chocolate and butter. Microwave on high power, stopping to stir every 20 seconds, just until the mixture is melted and smooth. Let cool completely.

Add the sugar to the chocolate mixture and whisk until blended. Whisk in the eggs one at a time, mixing after each addition until incorporated. Whisk in the vanilla, peppermint extract, and salt. Using a rubber spatula, fold in the flour and chocolate chips just until no white streaks remain. Do not overmix.

Divide the batter evenly among the prepared muffin cups. Bake until the tops are crackly and a toothpick inserted into the center of a cupcake comes out with only a few crumbs attached, 18–20 minutes. Let cool in the pan on a wire rack for 10 minutes, then carefully transfer the cupcakes directly to the rack and let cool completely, about 1 hour.

Using a small offset spatula or a butter knife, or a piping bag fitted with a star tip, top the cupcakes with the frosting. Decorate with chocolate mint candies and mint leaves, if using.

Coconut-Lime Cupcakes

Here, lime and coconut cupcakes are topped with Cream Cheese Frosting and plenty of toasted coconut. To make these extra lime-licious, before frosting, use a small knife to cut out a round 1½ inches in diameter and about 1 inch deep from the center of each cupcake and fill the hollow with a spoonful of Lime Curd (page 145), then frost as directed.

MAKES 12 CUPCAKES

1¾ cups all-purpose flour

2 teaspoons baking powder

¼ teaspoon salt

1 cup sugar

½ cup (1 stick) unsalted butter, at room temperature

1 tablespoon finely grated lime zest

3 large eggs, separated

1 teaspoon vanilla extract

½ cup coconut milk

1¾ cups sweetened dried coconut flakes, toasted (see Note)

Cream Cheese Frosting (page 140)

Preheat the oven to 350°F (180°C). Line 12 standard muffin cups with paper liners.

In a medium bowl, sift together the flour, baking powder, and salt. In a large bowl, using an electric mixer, beat together the sugar, butter, and lime zest on medium-high speed until pale and fluffy, about 3 minutes. Beat in the egg yolks one at a time, beating after each addition until incorporated. Add the vanilla and beat until blended. On low speed, add the flour mixture in three additions alternately with the coconut milk in two additions, beginning and ending with the flour mixture and beating just until blended after each addition. As you work, stop the mixer and scrape down the bowl with a rubber spatula as needed.

In another medium bowl, using the electric mixer with clean beaters, beat the egg whites on high speed until soft peaks form. Using a rubber spatula, stir one-fourth of the whites into the batter to lighten it. Pile the remaining whites on top of the batter and fold them in, leaving some white streaks visible. Finally, gently fold in 1 cup of the coconut flakes just until evenly distributed.

Divide the batter evenly among the prepared muffin cups, filling each one about three-fourths full. Bake until a toothpick inserted into the center comes out clean, about 20 minutes. Let cool in the pan on a wire rack for 5 minutes, then carefully transfer the cupcakes directly to the rack and let cool completely.

Stir ½ cup of the coconut flakes into the frosting. Using a small offset spatula, spread the frosting on the cupcakes, then sprinkle with more coconut.

Crunchy Coconut
To toast coconut, preheat the oven to 325°F. Spread the coconut on a baking sheet and bake, stirring once or twice, until lightly golden, about 5 minutes. Let cool before using.

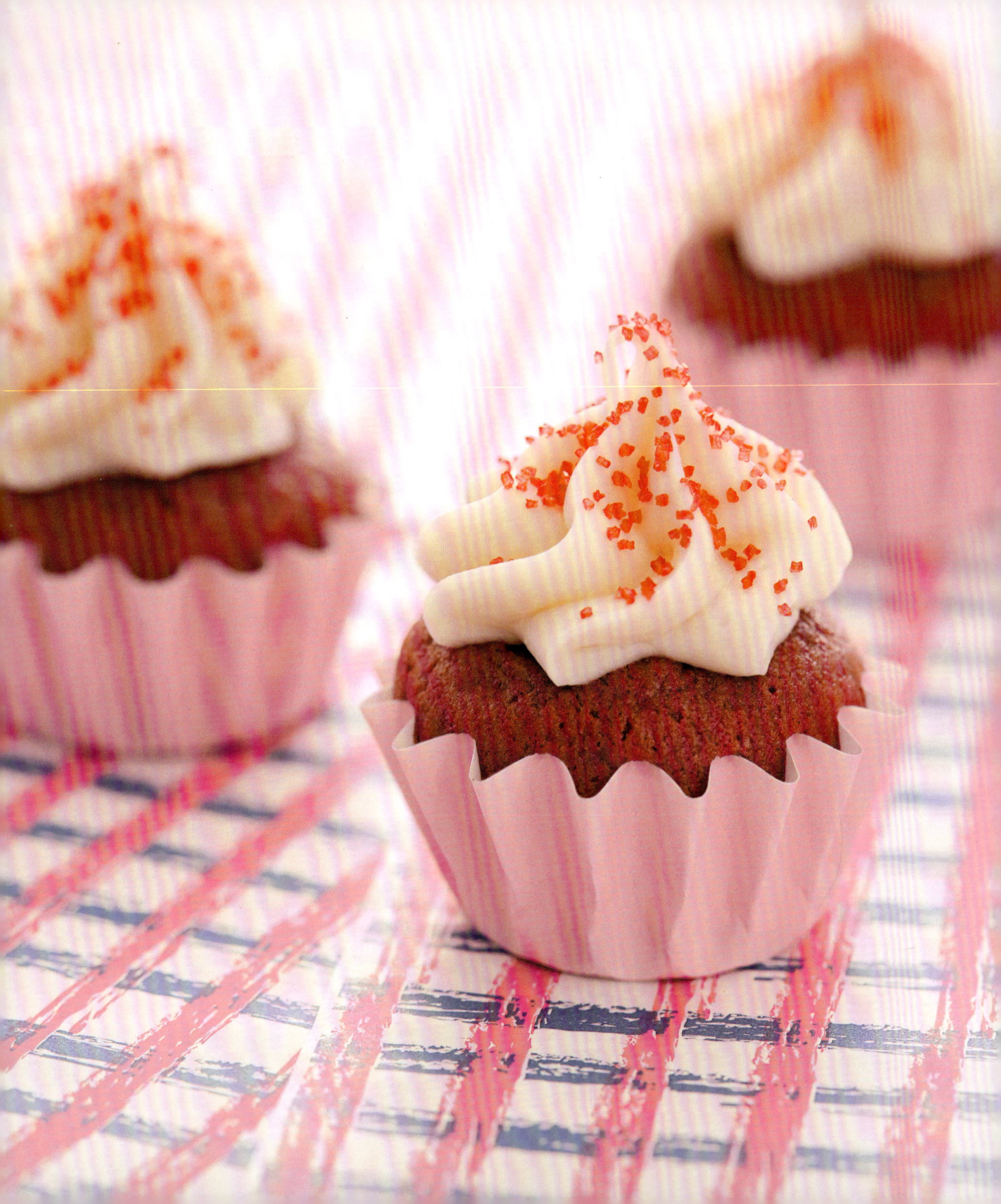

Mini Red Velvet Cupcakes with Cream Cheese Frosting

A favorite dessert offering in the South, red velvet cake has a fluffy texture and a mild cocoa flavor. It gets a little tang from the addition of buttermilk and vinegar, and it owes its traditional red tint to food coloring. For a more natural version, use beet powder or beet juice instead of food coloring.

MAKES 24 MINI CUPCAKES

1¼ cups cake flour

2 tablespoons unsweetened natural cocoa powder

¾ teaspoon baking powder

¼ teaspoon salt

½ cup buttermilk

1 teaspoon vanilla extract

½ teaspoon distilled white vinegar

4 drops red gel food coloring

¾ cup sugar

4 tablespoons (½ stick) unsalted butter, at cool room temperature

1 large egg, at room temperature

Cream Cheese Frosting (page 140)

Red sparkle sugar or sprinkles, for decorating

Preheat the oven to 350°F. Line 24 mini muffin cups with paper liners.

In a medium bowl, sift together the flour, cocoa powder, baking powder, and salt. In a small bowl, whisk together the buttermilk, vanilla, vinegar, and food coloring. In a large bowl, using an electric mixer, beat together the sugar and butter on medium-high speed until pale and fluffy, about 2 minutes. Add the egg and beat until incorporated. On low speed, add the flour mixture in three additions alternately with the buttermilk mixture in two additions, beginning and ending with the flour mixture and beating just until blended after each addition. As you work, stop the mixer to scrape down the bowl with a rubber spatula as needed.

Divide the batter evenly among the prepared muffin cups, filling each one about three-fourths full. Bake until a toothpick inserted into the center of a cupcake comes out clean, about 15 minutes. Let cool in the pan on a wire rack for about 5 minutes, then carefully transfer the cupcakes directly to the rack and let cool completely, about 30 minutes.

Spoon the frosting into a piping bag fitted with a ½-inch open or closed star tip and pipe decoratively onto the cupcakes. Decorate with sparkle sugar.

Blackberry Cheesecake Cupcakes

Creamy individual cheesecakes are swirled with blackberry jam for a purple-rific birthday treat. You can make these into strawberry or raspberry cheesecakes by swapping out the jam. Garnish with fresh berries of whichever jam you choose.

MAKES 16 CUPCAKES

FOR THE CRUST

⅔ cup graham cracker crumbs (from about 6 whole crackers)

2 teaspoons granulated sugar

3 tablespoons unsalted butter, melted

Pinch of salt

FOR THE FILLING

½ cup blackberry jam

Fresh lemon juice

1 pound cream cheese, at room temperature

⅔ cup granulated sugar

¼ cup sour cream

1 teaspoon vanilla extract

2 large eggs

1 tablespoon all-purpose flour

16 blackberries, for garnish

Powdered sugar, for dusting

Preheat the oven to 325°F. Line 16 standard muffin cups with paper liners.

To make the crust, in a bowl, using a fork, stir together the graham cracker crumbs, granulated sugar, butter, and salt until well mixed and evenly moistened. Divide the mixture evenly among the prepared muffin cups, pressing it onto the bottom of each cup. Bake until lightly golden, about 4 minutes. Let cool on a wire rack.

To make the filling, in a food processor, process the jam until smooth. If the jam is thick, add a little lemon juice to thin it until it has the consistency of a sauce. Scrape into a small bowl and set aside. Clean the processor bowl.

In the food processor, process the cream cheese until smooth, about 3 minutes. Add the granulated sugar and process until smooth, about 30 seconds. Stop the processor and scrape down the bowl with a rubber spatula. Add the sour cream and vanilla and process until well mixed. Add the eggs one at a time, processing after each addition until incorporated. Add the flour and process until mixed. Stop the processor, scrape down the bowl, and then process until well blended and smooth.

Divide the filling evenly among the prepared muffin cups, filling each cup three-fourths full. Top each cup with an equal amount of the jam, then use a toothpick to swirl the jam and cream cheese mixture together, creating a marbled pattern. Bake the cupcakes until they puff and are set, about 23 minutes. Let cool completely in the pans on wire racks. Cover with plastic wrap and refrigerate until chilled, at least 3 hours or up to overnight.

To serve, carefully remove the cupcakes from the pans. Top each cupcake with a blackberry. Using a fine-mesh sieve, dust the tops with powdered sugar.

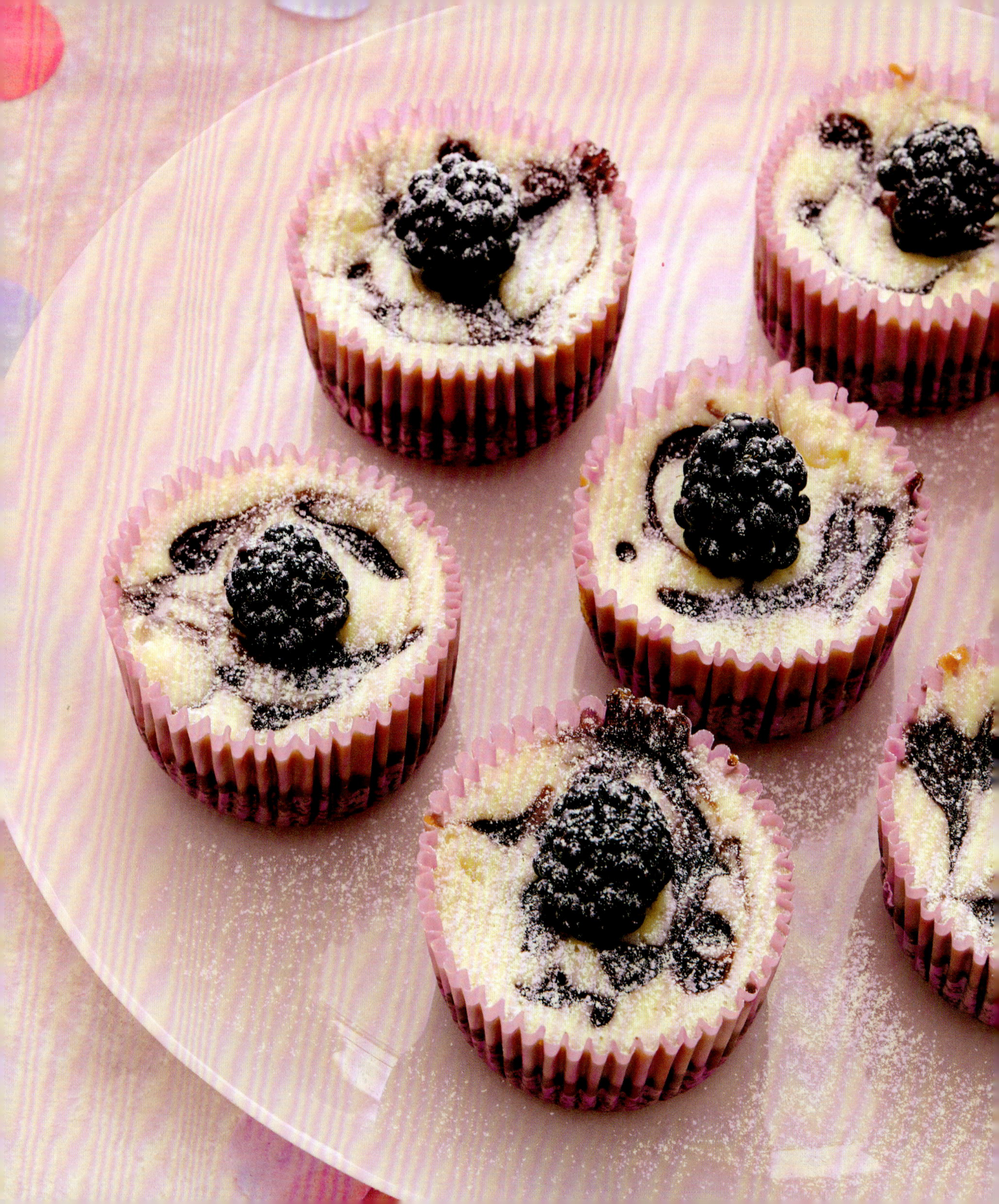

Frozen Treats

Recipe Note
To toast the almonds, preheat the oven to 325°F. Spread the almonds on a small baking sheet and bake, stirring once or twice, until lightly golden, 5–10 minutes. Let cool before using.

Dulce de Leche Ice Cream Pie

If you like ice cream, you are going to love this dessert. Gooey dulce de leche—a rich, milky, caramel-like sauce—is layered on a crunchy gingersnap cookie crust with ice cream, toasty almonds, and clouds of whipped cream. Use this method to create your own favorite combination by changing up the cookie crumbs and ice cream flavor.

MAKES 8–10 SERVINGS

1¼ cups gingersnap cookie crumbs

5 tablespoons unsalted butter, melted

3 tablespoons sugar

1 cup store-bought dulce de leche

1 quart vanilla ice cream, softened

¼ cup coarsely chopped natural almonds, toasted (see Note)

Whipped Cream (page 140)

Preheat the oven to 350°F. In a bowl, using a fork, stir together the crumbs, melted butter, and sugar until well mixed and the crumbs are evenly moistened. Turn the mixture out into a 9-inch pe pan or pie dish and pat the mixture firmly and evenly onto the bottom and up the sides. Bake the crust until firm, about 5 minutes. Let cool completely on a wire rack.

In a small saucepan over low heat, warm ¼ cup of the dulce de leche until it is spreadable but not hot. Remove from the heat and spread evenly over the bottom of the cooled crust. Cover and refrigerate until well chilled, about 1 hour.

In a large bowl, using an electric mixer, beat the ice cream on medium speed until spreadable but not runny. Pour ½ cup of the dulce de leche into the ice cream and swirl in with a spoon. Immediately mound the filling in the pie shell and spread evenly. Cover the pie and freeze until completely firm, 3–4 hours.

Just before serving, in a small saucepan over low heat, warm the remaining ¼ cup dulce de leche just until fluid but not hot. Working quickly, garnish the pie with the whipped cream, spreading it on top with an offset spatula and then piping swirls around the edge with a piping bag fitted with an open star tip. Drizzle the dulce de leche over the cream in an attractive pattern and finish with the nuts. Serve right away.

Ice Cream Sandwiches

A thick layer of creamy ice cream sits between thin, homemade chocolate wafer cookies in these better-than-bought ice cream sandwiches. A great make-ahead dessert for a party, they are easily personalized by your choice of ice cream flavor and decorations.

MAKES 6 SANDWICHES

½ cup (1 stick) unsalted butter, plus more for the pans

1¼ cups firmly packed dark brown sugar

3 ounces unsweetened chocolate, coarsely chopped

1 large egg

2 teaspoons vanilla extract

1¼ cups all-purpose flour

¾ teaspoon baking soda

¼ teaspoon salt

1½ pints ice cream of choice, slightly softened

About ½ cup mini chocolate chips, mini chocolate candies, sprinkles, and/or chopped toasted nuts, for decorating

In a heavy medium saucepan over low heat, combine the butter, brown sugar, and chopped chocolate and heat, stirring frequently, until the butter and chocolate melt, the sugar dissolves, and the mixture is smooth. Transfer to a heatproof medium bowl and let cool to lukewarm.

Add the egg and vanilla to the chocolate mixture and whisk until smooth. In another medium bowl, whisk together the flour, baking soda, and salt. Add the flour mixture to the chocolate mixture and stir until just until incorporated. Cover and refrigerate until firm, about 30 minutes. Preheat the oven to 350°F. Lightly butter 2 rimmed baking sheets.

Drop the dough by tablespoonfuls onto the prepared pans, spacing them at least 3 inches apart. You should have 12 cookies total. With dampened fingers, smooth the cookies into slightly flattened rounds about 3 inches in diameter. Bake until the edges darken and the centers are still slightly soft to the touch, about 10 minutes. Transfer the cookies to wire racks and let cool.

Lay half of the cookies, flat side up, on a work surface. Scoop about ½ cup of the ice cream onto each cookie and spread it to the edges. Top each one with a second cookie, flat side down. Using a small offset spatula, smooth the sides of each sandwich. Wrap each sandwich in plastic wrap. Lay the sandwiches on a clean, dry rimmed baking sheet and freeze until firm, at least 2 hours or up to 3 days.

When ready to serve, spread the decorations on a flat plate (or multiple plates) and carefully but firmly roll the edge of each ice cream sandwich in the decorations so they stick to the ice cream. Serve right away.

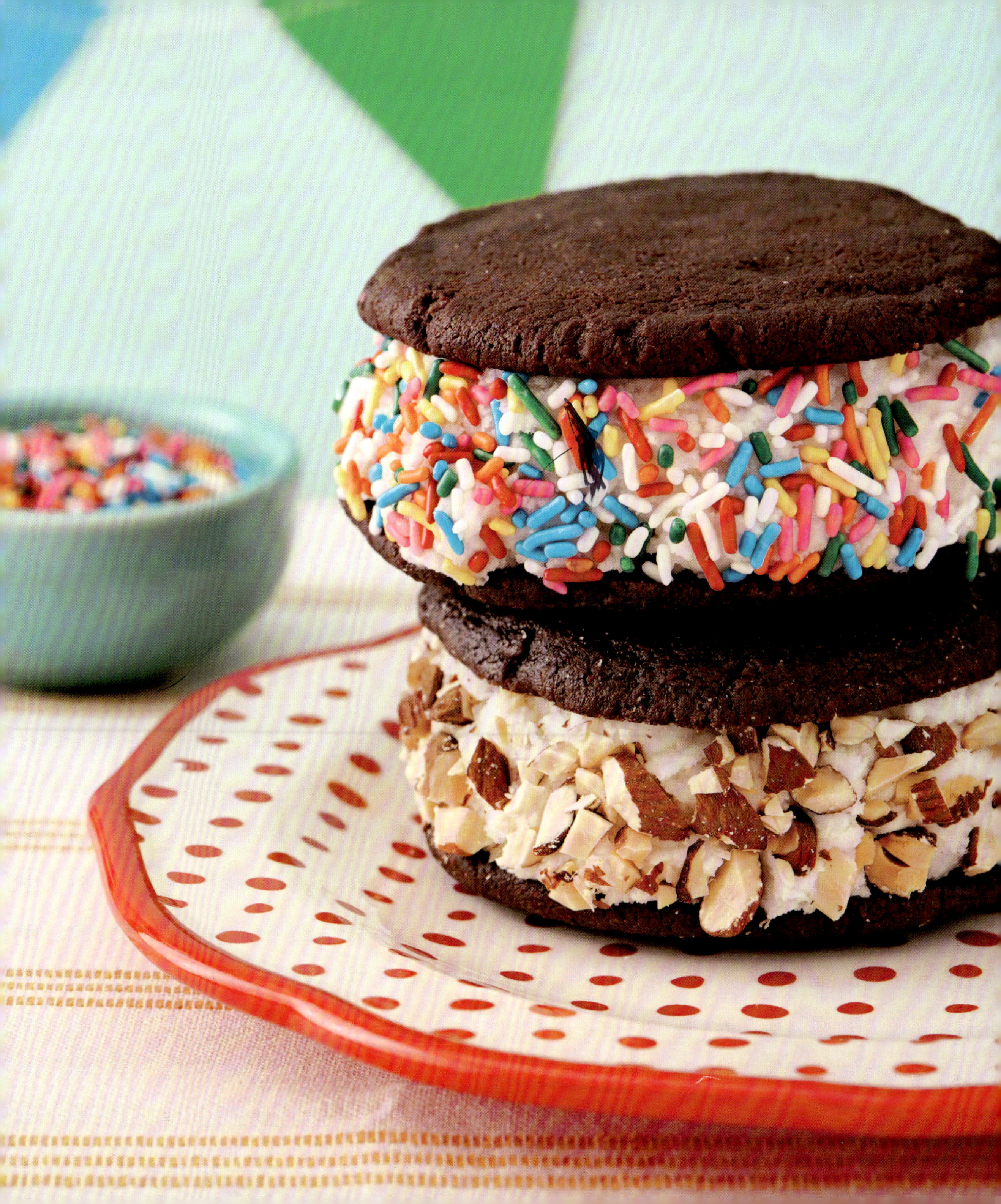

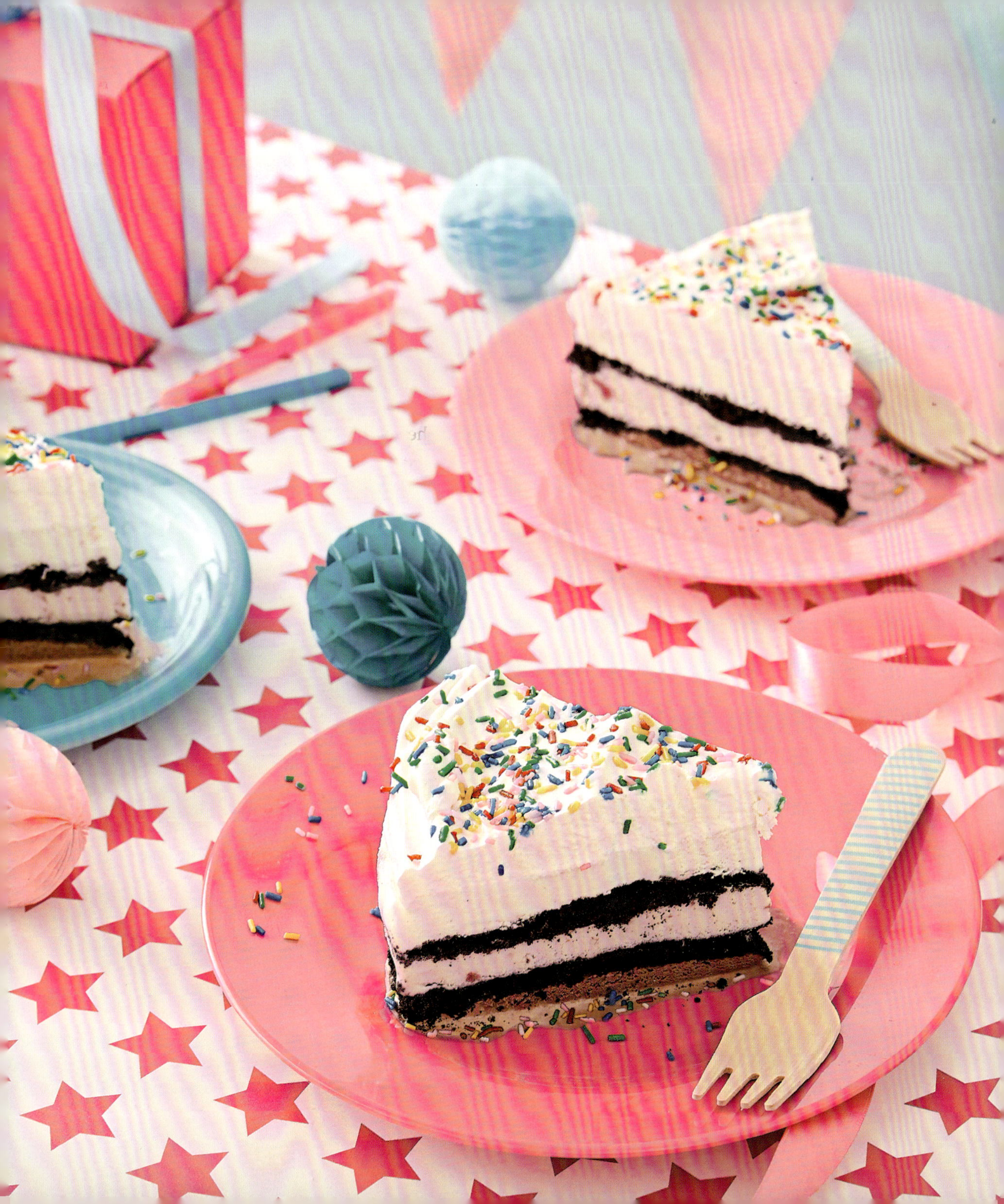

Any-Kind-of-Ice-Cream Birthday Cake

This make-ahead cake looks almost like a giant ice cream sundae. A thick layer of chocolate cake is topped with your favorite ice cream and then frosted with fluffy whipped cream. It can be made up to this point a day or two ahead and then glazed with the chocolate and decorated with sprinkles just before serving.

MAKES 12–16 SERVINGS

FOR THE CHOCOLATE CAKE

¼ cup canola oil, plus more for the pan

1¼ cups all-purpose flour

½ cup unsweetened natural cocoa powder

¾ teaspoon baking powder

¾ teaspoon baking soda

½ teaspoon salt

1 cup sugar

1 large whole egg plus 1 large egg yolk

¾ cup buttermilk

2 teaspoons vanilla extract

3 ounces semisweet chocolate chips, melted and cooled

½ teaspoon espresso powder

To make the cake, preheat the oven to 350°F. Grease the bottom and sides of a 9-inch springform pan with oil, line the bottom of the pan with parchment paper, and then oil the parchment.

In a medium bowl, sift together the flour, cocoa powder, baking powder, baking soda, and salt. In a stand mixer fitted with the paddle attachment, beat together the sugar, oil, whole egg, egg yolk, buttermilk, and vanilla on medium speed well blended and smooth, about 2 minutes. On low speed, slowly add the flour mixture and beat just until blended, stopping the mixer to scrape down the bowl with a rubber spatula as needed. Add the melted chocolate and espresso powder and beat just until blended. Then increase the speed to high and beat for 20 seconds.

Pour the batter into the prepared pan and spread evenly. Bake the cake until a toothpick inserted into the center comes out clean, 28–30 minutes. Let the cake cool in the pan on a wire rack for 20 minutes. Release the pan sides, opening them widely so they fall away from the cake. Invert the cake onto the wire rack, remove the base, and peel off the parchment. Turn the cake top side up and let cool completely.

Continued on page 80

~ *Continued from page 79* ~

FOR THE FILLING AND TOPPING

1 quart ice cream of choice, softened just until spreadable

1½ cups heavy cream

¾ cup powdered sugar

½ teaspoon vanilla extract

FOR THE CHOCOLATE TOPPING (OPTIONAL)

¾ cup heavy cream

6 ounces bittersweet chocolate, coarsely chopped

Rainbow sprinkles, for decorating

To assemble the cake, rinse and dry the springform pan, then line the sides with parchment paper so the parchment extends about 4 inches above the rim of the pan. Using a long serrated knife and a sawing motion, cut the cooled cake in half horizontally. Place the bottom half, cut side up, in the pan. Spread the ice cream over the cake in an even layer. Place the top half of the cake, cut side down, on the ice cream layer. Freeze for at least 6 hours or up to overnight.

At least 1 hour before serving, make the frosting. In the stand mixer fitted with the whisk attachment, beat together the cream, powdered sugar, and vanilla on medium-high speed until stiff peaks form, about 3 minutes. Remove the cake from the freezer, release the pan sides, and discard the parchment. Transfer the cake to a serving plate. Using an offset spatula, spread the frosting over the top of the cake in a thick, even layer. Freeze until ready to serve, at least 1 hour or up to 3 days. (Once the cake is frozen, it can be covered with plastic wrap and returned to the freezer.)

Just before serving, make the chocolate topping, if using. In a small saucepan over medium heat, warm the heavy cream until steaming hot but not boiling. Put the bittersweet chocolate into a heatproof bowl and pour the hot cream over the chocolate. Let stand for 5 minutes, then whisk gently until smooth. Let cool slightly.

To serve, remove the cake from the freezer and pour the chocolate mixture (if using) over the top, allowing some of it to drip over the sides. Because the cake is frozen, the topping will set quickly. Decorate the top of the cake with sprinkles and serve right away. Leftover cake can be wrapped in plastic wrap and stored in the freezer for up to 3 days.

Profiteroles with Ice Cream and Chocolate Sauce

Profiteroles are small, delicate puffs made from a light pastry called choux. They can be filled with ice cream in any flavor you love and then drizzled with chocolate sauce, or you can spoon vanilla or chocolate pudding into the center and dip the top in Chocolate Glaze (page 144).

MAKES 10–12 SERVINGS

½ cup whole milk

½ cup water

6 tablespoons (¾ stick) unsalted butter, cut into tablespoon-size pieces

¼ teaspoon salt

1 cup all-purpose flour

4 large eggs

1 quart ice cream, such as salted caramel, chocolate, vanilla, or your favorite flavor

Chocolate Sauce (page 145)

In a saucepan over medium-high heat, combine the milk, water, butter, and salt and bring to a full boil. When the butter melts, remove the pan from the heat, add the flour all at once, and stir vigorously with a wooden spoon until blended. Return the pan to medium heat and continue stirring until the mixture leaves the sides of the pan and forms a ball. Remove from the heat and let cool for 3–4 minutes, or until an instant-read thermometer inserted into the center of the ball registers 140°F.

In a small bowl, whisk 1 egg. When the batter has cooled, pour the whisked egg into the batter and beat with the spoon until incorporated. Add the remaining 3 eggs one at a time, first whisking each one and then beating it into the batter. After each egg is added, the mixture will separate and appear shiny, but it will return to a smooth paste with vigorous beating. Let the paste cool for 10 minutes.

Position 2 racks in the center of the oven and preheat the oven to 425°F. Line the bottoms of 2 rimmed baking sheets with parchment paper.

Continued on page 82

> **A French Fete**
> Garnish the profiteroles with little French flags, decorate with streamers, and serve petite bottles of sparkling French lemonade.

~ *Continued from page 81* ~

Spoon the paste into a piping bag with a $^3/_{16}$-inch round tip. For each small puff, pipe about 1 teaspoon paste onto a prepared pan, forming a mound ½ inch in diameter and spacing the mounds at least 2 inches apart. You should have about 40 puffs.

Bake the puffs for 15 minutes, then reduce the heat to 375°F and continue baking until golden brown, 5–10 minutes longer. Do not open the oven door for the first 20 minutes of baking. Remove from the oven and immediately prick the side of each puff with the tip of a sharp knife. Return the pans to the oven, leave the oven door ajar, and allow the puffs to dry out for about 15 minutes. Let the puffs cool completely on the pans on wire racks.

To serve, slit each puff in half horizontally almost all the way through. Fill each puff with a small scoop of ice cream. Arrange the filled puffs on individual plates and top with the sauce.

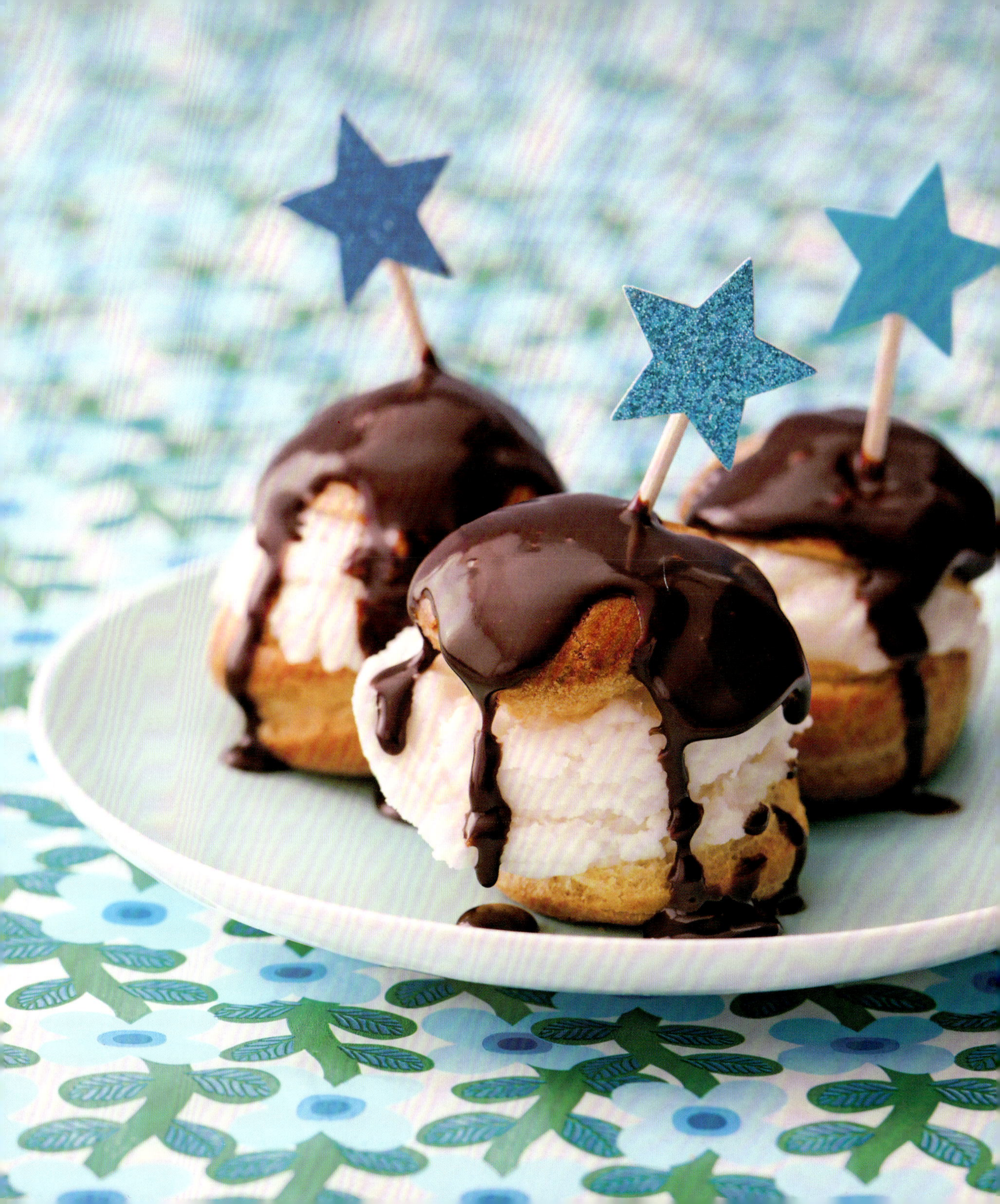

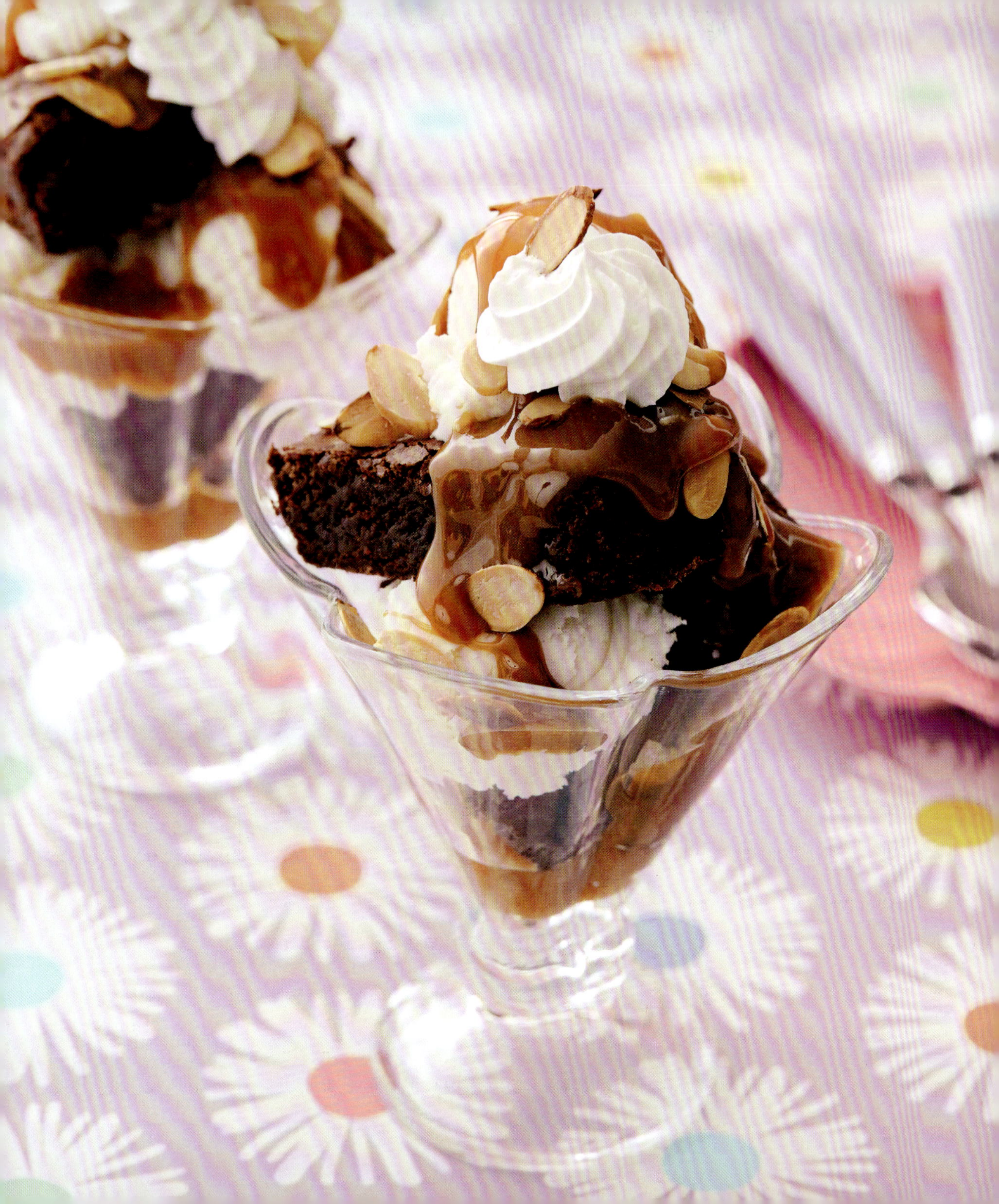

Chocolate-Caramel Brownie Ice Cream Sundaes

A build-it-yourself sundae bar is a fun time at any party. Set out brownies, two or three kinds of ice cream, a bowl of whipped cream, and an array of sauces and garnishes and let your guests put together their own delicious dessert.

MAKES 6 SUNDAES

FOR THE BROWNIES

6 ounces unsweetened chocolate, chopped

¾ cup (1½ sticks) unsalted butter, cut into several pieces

3 large eggs

1¾ cups sugar

¼ teaspoon salt

2 teaspoons vanilla extract

1 cup plus 2 tablespoons all-purpose flour

About 1½ cups store-bought caramel sauce, warmed until pourable

1 quart vanilla, chocolate, or salted caramel ice cream

Whipped Cream (page 140)

Sliced almonds, toasted, or chocolate sprinkles, for garnish

To make the brownies, preheat the oven to 350°F. Butter the bottom and sides of an 8-inch square baking pan.

Fill a medium saucepan one-third full with water and heat until barely simmering over medium-low heat. Rest a heatproof bowl in the rim of the saucepan over (not touching) the water, add the chocolate and butter, and heat, stirring often, until the chocolate and butter have melted and the mixture is smooth, about 4 minutes. Turn off the heat, remove the bowl, and let the chocolate mixture cool slightly.

In a large bowl, whisk together the eggs, sugar, salt, and vanilla until well blended. Whisk in the chocolate mixture until blended. Sprinkle the flour over the top and whisk slowly just until well mixed.

Pour the batter into the prepared pan, spreading it evenly. Bake until a toothpick inserted into the center comes out almost clean or with a few moist crumbs clinging to it, 35–40 minutes. Be careful not to overbake. Let cool completely in the pan on a wire rack, about 1 hour. Cut into 12 equal pieces.

To assemble the sundaes, arrange a brownie in each of 6 individual bowls and drizzle with 1–2 tablespoons of the caramel sauce. Top each serving with a scoop of ice cream, followed by another brownie, another scoop of ice cream, and 2–3 more tablespoons sauce. Dollop each serving with whipped cream, then garnish with almonds. Serve right away.

Chocolate-Mint Mini Ice Cream Cakes

Individual ice cream cakelets make for a celebration. Half-sized chocolate cupcakes are baked, cooled, topped with minty ice cream, frozen, and then finished with a swirl of whipped cream. Change the flavor of the ice cream if you like. Coffee or salted caramel would be great here.

MAKES 18 CAKES

FOR THE CAKES

1 cup all-purpose flour

¼ cup Dutch-process cocoa powder

2 teaspoons baking powder

¼ teaspoon salt

⅔ cup sugar

¾ cup warm water

2 large eggs

½ cup avocado or canola oil

½ teaspoon mint extract

I quart mint chip ice cream, slightly softened

Whipped Cream (page 140)

Chocolate sprinkles or mini chocolate chips, for decorating (optional)

Preheat the oven to 325°F. Line 18 standard muffin cups with paper or foil liners.

To make the cakes, in a large bowl, sift together the flour, cocoa, baking powder, and salt. Whisk in the sugar. In a medium bowl, whisk together the warm water, eggs, oil, and mint extract until blended. Pour the egg mixture into the flour mixture and stir with the whisk just until blended.

Divide the batter evenly among the prepared muffin cups. Bake until a toothpick inserted into the center of a cupcake comes out clean, about 10 minutes. Let cool in the pans on wire racks for 5 minutes, then carefully transfer the cupcakes directly to the racks and let cool completely. Set the muffin pans aside to cool.

Return the cupcakes to the cooled muffin pans. Put the ice cream into a bowl and stir with a large metal spoon until spreadable. Drop a big spoonful of the ice cream over the top of each cupcake, filling the cup and spreading it in an even layer. Cover the pans with plastic wrap and freeze the cupcakes until firm, about 2 hours.

Spoon the whipped cream into a piping bag fitted with a small open star tip and pipe decoratively onto each frozen cupcake. Alternatively, using a small offset spatula, spread the whipped cream onto each frozen cupcake. Top with sprinkles, if using. Serve right away.

Dreamy Orange and Vanilla Ice-Cream Pops

With only two ingredients, these classically flavored ice-cream pops couldn't be simpler. You'll need an ice-pop mold for the traditional shape, but they can also be made in a baking pan and cut into rectangles.

MAKES 8–10 ICE-CREAM POPS

1 quart vanilla ice cream, softened

½ cup frozen orange juice concentrate, partially thawed

In a bowl, using a spoon, swirl together the ice cream and orange juice concentrate until barely blended.

Spoon the mixture into ice-pop molds, dividing it evenly. Insert the sticks. Freeze the ice pops for at least 8 hours or up to overnight. To serve, run the molds under warm water for 30 seconds to release the pops.

Alternatively, line an 8-inch square baking pan with plastic wrap, allowing a 5-inch overhang on two sides. Spoon the ice cream mixture into the prepared pan, spreading it evenly, and bring the plastic wrap up over the top to cover. Freeze overnight. The next day, cut the frozen ice cream into 10 rectangles. Using a small offset spatula, lift out each rectangle and insert a wooden pop stick into one end. If the pops have softened, lay them on a rimmed baking sheet and return them to the freezer until they firm up. Serve directly from the baking sheet, or wrap each pop in waxed paper, twist the paper where the pop meets the stick, and freeze until ready to serve.

Watermelon-Mint Ice Pops

When you are looking for a refreshing treat for a summer birthday, look no further than these fruity ice pops. You can use this same method for other fruits as well. Try hulled strawberries, peeled and sliced peaches, or mixed berries.

MAKES 8–10 ICE POPS

4½ cups seedless watermelon chunks

½ cup sugar

Pinch of salt

1 teaspoon chopped fresh mint leaves

In a blender, combine the watermelon, sugar, salt, and mint and process until the sugar dissolves and the mixture is liquid. It's fine if small pieces of watermelon remain.

Pour the watermelon mixture into a glass measuring cup with a spout. Divide the mixture evenly among ice-pop molds. Insert the sticks. Freeze the ice pops for at least 8 hours or up to overnight.

To serve, run the molds under warm water for 30 seconds to release the ice pops.

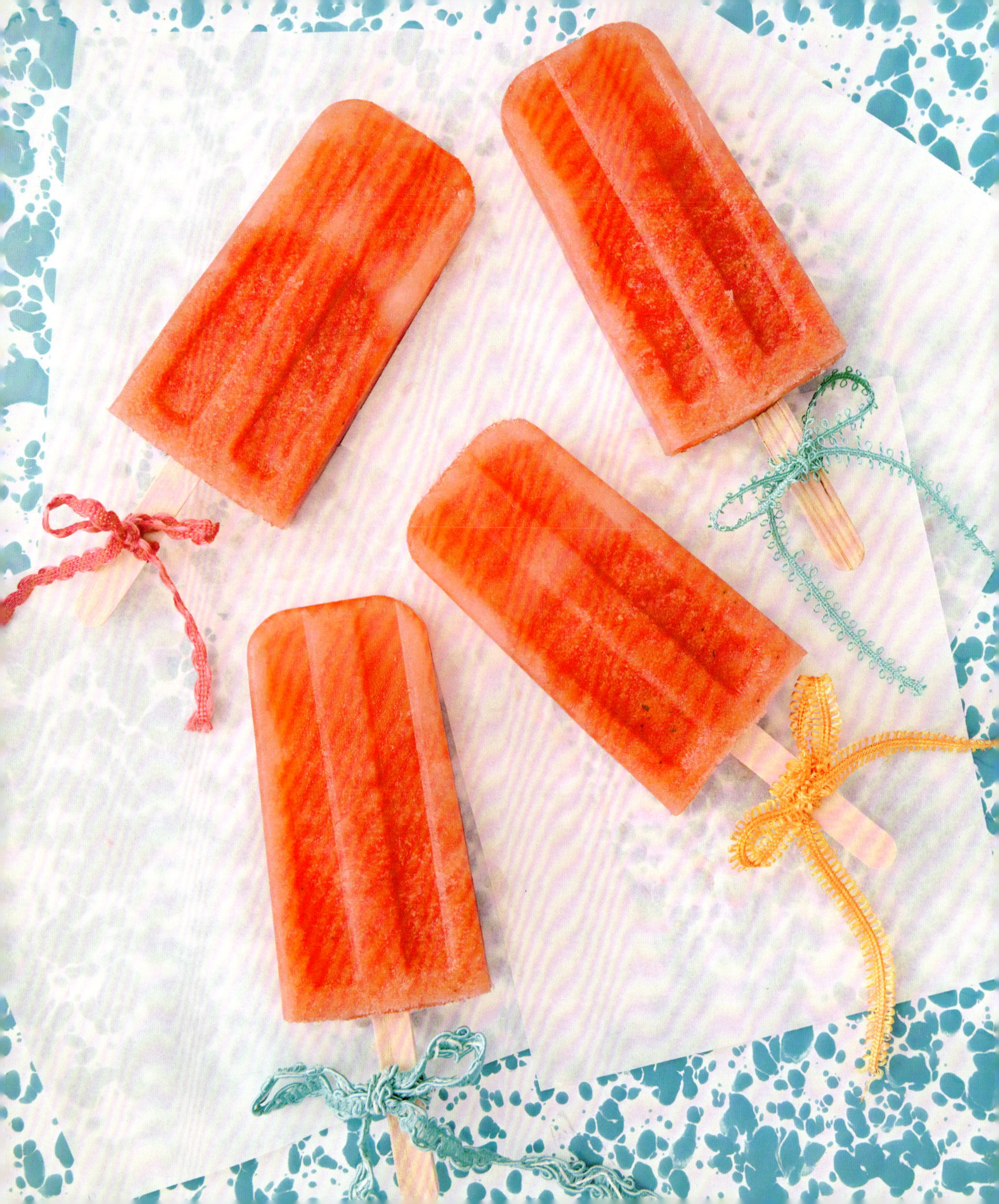

Pies and Tarts

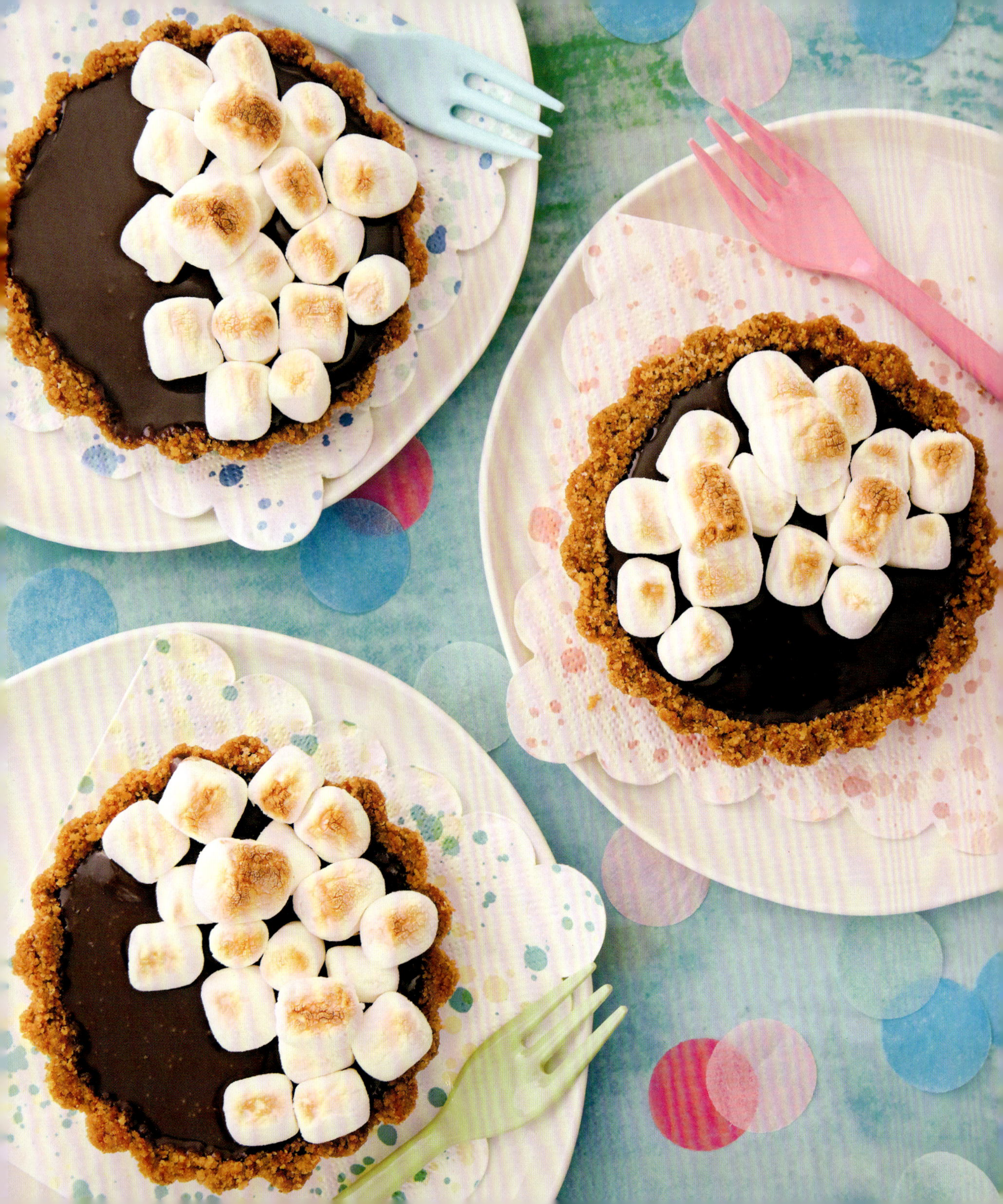

S'mores Tartlets

Ooey, gooey s'mores are a campout treat. But you don't have to be out in the wilderness to enjoy the decadent marriage of marshmallow, chocolate, and graham crackers. Don't have tartlet pans? Make these in a muffin pan instead! Just line 6 to 8 muffin cups with paper liners, then divide the crust and filling evenly among the cups.

MAKES 6 TARTLETS

FOR THE CRUST

9 whole graham crackers, finely crushed

6 tablespoons (¾ stick) unsalted butter, melted and cooled

2 tablespoons firmly packed dark brown sugar

FOR THE FILLING

1 cup milk chocolate chips

2 tablespoons unsalted butter, at room temperature

½ cup heavy cream

1 tablespoon granulated sugar

¼ teaspoon salt

1½ cups miniature marshmallows

To make the crust, preheat the oven to 350°F. In a food processor, process the graham crackers to fine crumbs. Transfer to a medium bowl, add the melted butter and brown sugar, and, using a fork, stir until well mixed and the crumbs are evenly moistened. Divide the mixture evenly among six 3½-inch tartlet pans with removable bottoms. Press evenly onto the bottom and up the sides of each pan. Place the pans on a rimmed baking sheet and freeze until firm, about 15 minutes.

Bake the crusts until lightly browned and set, about 10 minutes. Transfer the baking sheet to a wire rack and let the crusts cool completely.

To make the filling, in a heatproof medium bowl, combine the chocolate chips and butter. In a small saucepan over medium heat, warm the cream just until it starts to simmer. Remove from the heat and pour over the chocolate chips and butter. Let stand until the chocolate starts to melt, about 3 minutes, then whisk until blended. Whisk in the granulated sugar and salt until they dissolve and the mixture is smooth.

Divide the chocolate mixture evenly among the tartlet crusts, filling them to just below the top edge of the crust. Cover with plastic wrap and refrigerate for at least 2 hours or up to 2 days.

Before serving, preheat the broiler. Unmold the tartlets and place on a rimmed baking sheet. Top with the marshmallows and broil until they are toasted, about 2 minutes. Let cool completely on a wire rack before serving.

Strawberry Mousse Pie

Rich with fresh strawberry flavor, this fluffy refrigerator pie requires the oven for only a few minutes. To save time, use a purchased graham cracker crust. Any leftover strawberry mousse filling can be poured into ramekins, topped with whipped cream, and served as a light dessert.

MAKES 6–8 SERVINGS

FOR THE CRUST

12 graham crackers

¼ cup granulated sugar

6 tablespoons (¾ stick) unsalted butter, melted and cooled

⅛ teaspoon salt

FOR THE FILLING

3 tablespoons water

1 tablespoon (1 package) unflavored gelatin powder

3 cups hulled and chopped strawberries (about 1¼ pounds berries)

1 tablespoon fresh lemon juice

4 ounces cream cheese, at room temperature

2 teaspoons vanilla extract

¾ cup powdered sugar

1½ cups cold heavy cream

To make the crust, preheat the oven to 350°F. In a food processor, process the graham crackers to fine crumbs. Transfer the crumbs to a medium bowl, add the granulated sugar, butter, and salt, and, using a fork, stir until well mixed and the crumbs are evenly moistened.

Dump the mixture into a 9-inch pie dish and press firmly and evenly onto the bottom and up the sides to the rim. A flat-bottomed glass is handy for pressing the crumb mixture so it sticks together. Bake the crust until set and golden brown, about 12 minutes. Let cool completely on a wire rack.

To make the filling, put the water into a small microwave-safe bowl, sprinkle the gelatin evenly over the top, and whisk gently to combine. Wipe out the food processor bowl. Add the strawberries and lemon juice and process until a purée forms. Pour the purée into a fine-mesh sieve set over a medium bowl. Using the back of a spoon or a rubber spatula, press against the purée, forcing as much liquid through the sieve as possible. Discard any seeds in the sieve.

Wipe out the food processor bowl. Add the cream cheese and vanilla and process until the cream cheese is softened. Add the powdered sugar and process until well blended. Scrape into a medium bowl.

Continued on page 96

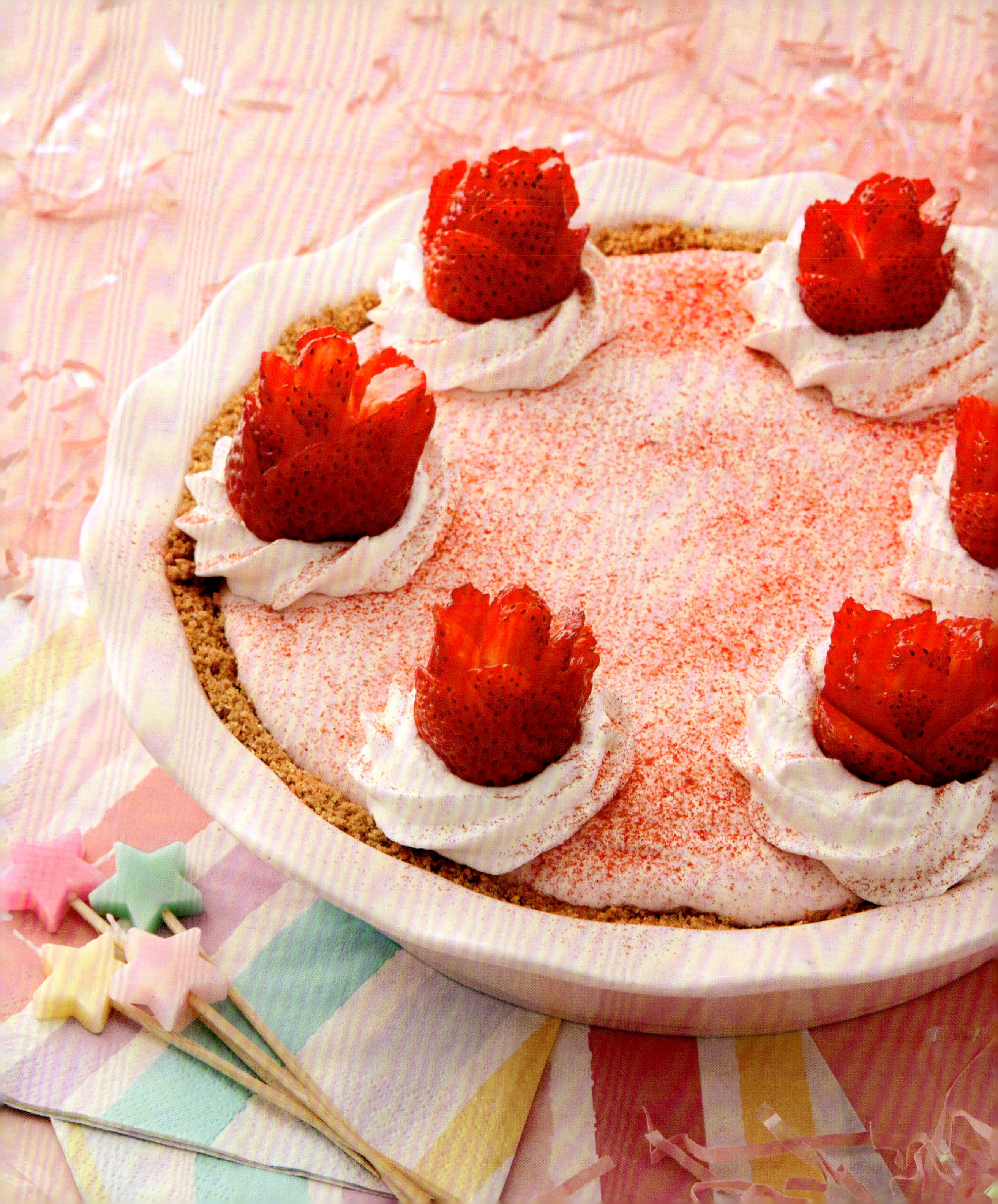

FOR DECORATING

1 cup Whipped Cream (page 140)

6–8 large Strawberry "Roses" (page 146), optional

Dehydrated strawberries, crushed to powder, for decorating (optional)

~ *Continued from page 94* ~

Add ¼ cup of the strawberry purée to the gelatin mixture. Microwave on high power just until hot, about 30 seconds, then whisk until the gelatin dissolves. Pour the gelatin mixture into the bowl with the remaining strawberry purée and stir to combine. Pour the strawberry mixture into the cream cheese mixture and whisk until evenly blended.

In a separate bowl, using a clean whisk, whip the cream to soft peaks. Gently fold the whipped cream into the strawberry–cream cheese mixture just until no white streaks are visible.

Pour the filling into the cooled crust and smooth the top. Cover with plastic wrap and refrigerate until set and chilled, about 2 hours.

To serve, spoon the whipped cream into a piping bag fitted with a star tip and pipe 6–8 large rosettes decoratively around the pie. If you like, top each rosette with a strawberry "rose," then dust the pie with the strawberry powder, if using. Serve right away.

Chocolate Raspberry Tartlets

These two-bite tartlets would be right at home at an afternoon birthday party. Their tender cocoa crust holds a zingy raspberry cream filling, which is finished with a fresh raspberry and a delicate dusting of sugar.

MAKES 12 TARTLETS

FOR THE TARTLET SHELLS

½ cup (1 stick) unsalted butter, at cool room temperature, cut into tablespoon-size pieces

⅓ cup powdered sugar, sifted

1 large egg yolk

1 teaspoon vanilla extract

¼ teaspoon salt

1¼ cups all-purpose flour, plus more for dusting

¼ cup unsweetened natural cocoa powder

Nonstick cooking spray, for the pan

FOR THE FILLING

1 cup heavy cream

2 tablespoons seedless raspberry jam

12 fresh raspberries, for garnish

Powdered sugar, for dusting

To make the tartlet shells, in a bowl, using an electric mixer, beat together the butter, sugar, egg yolk, vanilla, and salt on medium-high speed until smooth, about 1 minute. Stop the mixer and scrape down the bowl with a rubber spatula. Sift together the flour and cocoa powder over the butter-sugar mixture. On low speed, beat just until the dry ingredients are evenly moistened and the mixture starts to clump together in a shaggy dough. If the dough seems too dry, add water 1 teaspoon at a time until the dough comes together. Turn the dough out onto a lightly floured work surface, bring it together, and press into a thick disk, Wrap the disk in plastic wrap and refrigerate for at least 30 minutes or up to overnight.

Lightly spray 12 standard muffin cups with cooking spray. On a lightly floured work surface, roll out the dough into a round about ⅛ inch thick. If the dough tears, press it back together. Using a 3¼-inch round fluted cookie cutter, cut out as many rounds as possible. Gather up the scraps, press them together, roll out, and cut out more rounds. You should have 12 rounds total. Transfer each round to a prepared muffin cup, gently pressing it onto the bottom and partway up the sides. Freeze until firm, about 30 minutes.

Preheat the oven to 350°F. Bake the tartlet shells until golden and cooked through, about 15 minutes. Let cool in the pan on a wire rack for 10 minutes, then carefully transfer the tartlet shells directly to the rack and let cool completely.

Continued on page 98

> **Afternoon Delight**
> Fancy a tea party for your birthday? Serve these tartlets on a tiered tray sprinkled with edible flowers and offer freshly brewed mint tisane in pretty teacups.

~ *Continued from page 97* ~

When the shells are cool, make the filling. In a medium bowl, using the electric mixer, beat together the cream and jam on medium-high speed until stiff peaks form, about 5 minutes. The peaks should stand straight when the beaters are lifted; be careful not to overwhip.

Spoon the filling into a piping bag fitted with a large open star tip and pipe into the tartlet shells, dividing it evenly. Top each tartlet with a raspberry. Using a fine-mesh sieve, dust the tops with sugar. Serve right away.

Little Cherry Galettes

A galette is a free-form, rustic tart. You can make individual galettes, like these, or a single large one. Prepare the cherry filling and pastry dough a day in advance, and then the galettes are easy to assemble and bake the day you serve them. Whipped cream is dreamy, but scoops of vanilla ice cream would be yummy too.

MAKES 10 INDIVIDUAL GALETTES

FOR THE FILLING

½ cup granulated sugar

3 tablespoons tapioca flour or cornstarch

3 cans (14½ ounces each) unsweetened pitted red tart cherries in water

1 tablespoon fresh lemon juice

Double recipe Flaky Pastry Dough (page 149)

1 large egg beaten with 1 teaspoon water, for egg wash

Sparkle sugar, for sprinkling

Whipped Cream (page 140), for serving (optional)

To make the filling, in a small bowl, using a fork, stir together the granulated sugar and tapioca flour. Drain the cherries into a fine-mesh sieve set over a bowl. Reserve ¼ cup of the liquid.

In a medium saucepan over medium heat, combine the cherries, the ¼ cup cherry liquid, the sugar mixture, and lemon juice and bring to a simmer, stirring constantly. Cook, stirring, until the juices thicken, about 5 minutes. Remove from the heat and let cool completely.

Prepare the dough as directed, divide in half, wrap in plastic wrap, and refrigerate for 30 minutes. Line the bottoms of 2 large rimmed baking sheets with parchment paper.

On a lightly floured surface, roll out half of the dough into a large round about ⅛ inch thick. Using a 7-inch round plate or other template and a small knife, cut out as many 7-inch rounds of dough as possible. Transfer the rounds to a clean work surface. Gather up the scraps and set aside. Repeat with the remaining dough half. Press together all the dough scraps, roll out the dough the same way, cut out additional dough rounds, and add to the clean work surface. You should have 10 rounds total.

~ Continued on page 101 ~

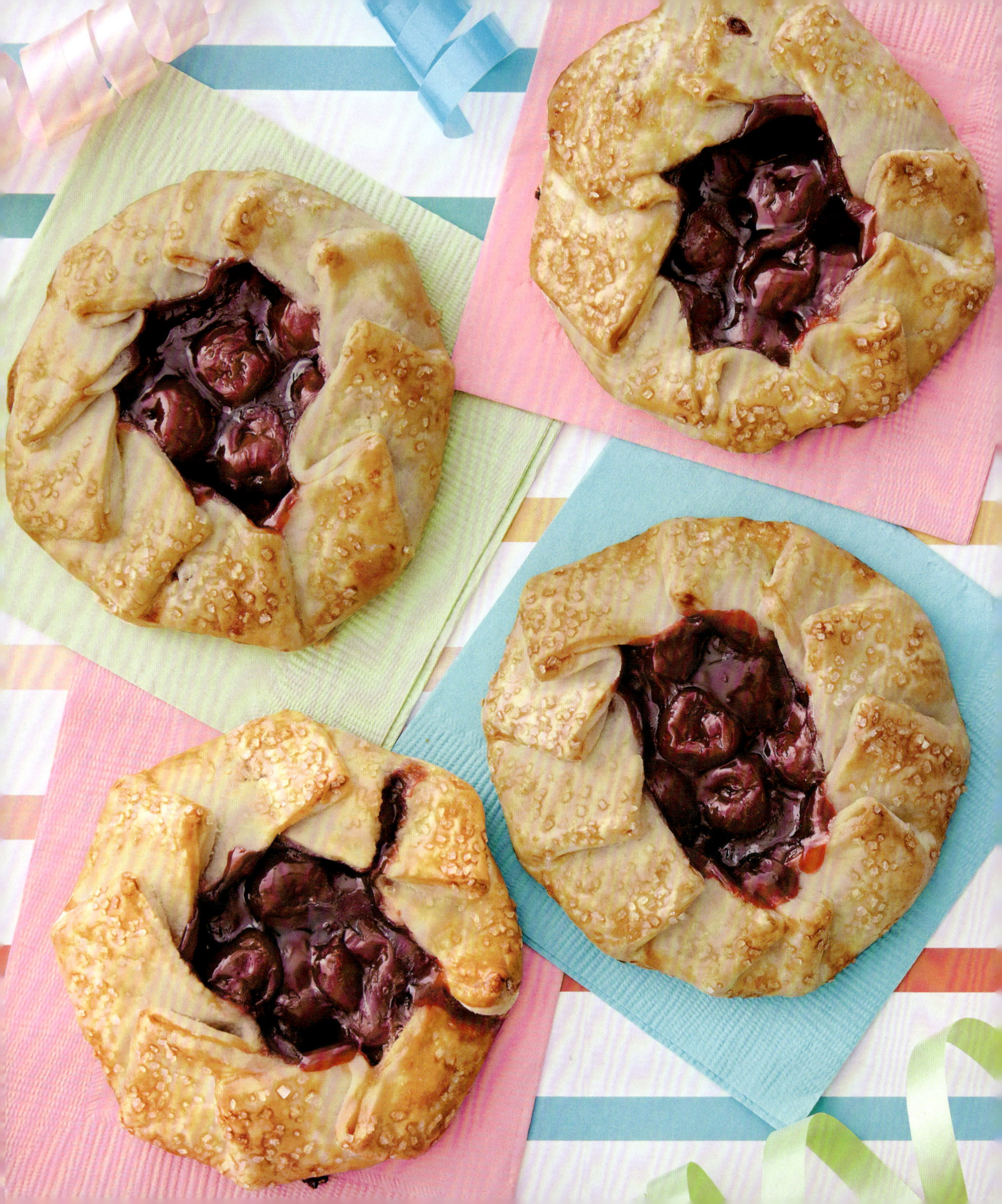

À La Mode

These petite galettes are even tastier with ice cream on top. Try a mix of flavors—salted caramel and cinnamon are delicious with the cherry filling.

~ *Continued from page 99* ~

Brush the dough rounds with some of the egg wash. Divide the cherry filling evenly among the rounds, placing it in a mound in the center of each round (about ¼ cup filling per round). Fold the edges of the dough up over the filling, forming pleats around the perimeter and leaving the center uncovered. Press the pleats firmly to hold together. Using a wide metal spatula, transfer the galettes to the prepared pans, dividing them evenly between the pans. Refrigerate for at least 15 minutes or up to 2 hours. About 15 minutes before you are ready to bake, position 2 racks in the center of the oven and preheat the oven to 400°F.

Lightly brush the pleated dough with the egg wash and sprinkle with sparkle sugar. Bake the galettes, switching the pans between the racks and rotating the pans back to front about halfway through baking, until the crust is golden brown and the filling is bubbling, about 30 minutes. Let the galettes cool on the pans on wire racks for at least a few minutes before serving.

Serve warm or at room temperature, topped with whipped cream, if desired.

Tropical Fruit Cream Tart

This sunny tart calls for a shortbread-like crust, a filling of thick, rich vanilla pastry cream (similar to pudding), and a colorful array of fresh fruits on top. The mango and kiwis give the tart its tropical flair, but you can also use mixed berries and sliced nectarines.

MAKES 6–8 SERVINGS

Tart Dough (page 149)

FOR THE PASTRY CREAM

1½ cups whole milk

4 large egg yolks

⅓ cup sugar

3 tablespoons cornstarch

⅛ teaspoon salt

1 teaspoon vanilla extract

1 ripe but firm mango, peeled, pitted, and sliced

2 cups hulled and sliced strawberries

2 kiwifruits, peeled and sliced crosswise

2 tablespoons apricot preserves

Prepare the dough and chill as directed. On a lightly floured work surface, roll out the dough into a round about 12 inches in diameter and about ⅛ inch thick. Transfer the round to a 9½-inch tart pan with removable bottom and ease it into the pan, patting it firmly onto the bottom and up the sides. Trim the edge even with the rim. Refrigerate or freeze until firm, about 30 minutes.

Preheat the oven to 375°F. Line the tart shell with aluminum foil and fill with pie weights. Bake the crust until it starts to look dry, about 15 minutes. Remove the weights and foil and continue baking until golden, about 15 minutes longer. Let cool completely on a wire rack.

To make the pastry cream, in a medium saucepan, warm the milk over medium heat until tiny bubbles start to appear along the pan edges. Remove from the heat. In a medium bowl, whisk together the egg yolks and sugar until pale yellow. Whisk in the cornstarch and salt. Gradually pour half of the hot milk into the yolk mixture while whisking constantly. Whisk in the remaining milk and then pour the mixture into the saucepan. Return the pan to medium heat and cook, whisking constantly, until the mixture thickens to a pudding-like consistency, 8–10 minutes. Do not let it boil.

> **Playtime!**
> *Arrange the fresh fruit on this colorful tart in a pretty pattern. Try a spiral, star, flower, or stripes—or spell out the birthday girl's name.*

Remove from the heat, scrape into a heatproof bowl, and whisk in the vanilla. Cover with plastic wrap, pressing it directly onto the surface of the pastry cream (to prevent a "skin" from forming), and poke a few holes in the plastic to allow steam to escape. Let cool for a few minutes, then refrigerate until chilled, 2–3 hours.

To assemble the tart, stir the chilled pastry cream until smooth. Spoon into the tart shell and spread evenly. Arrange the mango, strawberry, and kiwi slices decoratively over the pasty cream. Spoon the apricot preserves into a small microwave-safe bowl and microwave on high power just until warm and melted. Strain through a medium-mesh sieve into a small bowl, then brush the fruit slices gently with the strained preserves. Let sit for a minute or two before serving.

Spiced Apple Rose Tartlets with Caramel

Making the apple roses takes a little practice, but the effect in the finished tartlets is worth the effort. You can make your own pie dough (it's a snap in a food processor) or use store-bought dough. If using purchased, look for a frozen all-butter dough and thaw it in the refrigerator.

MAKES 12 TARTLETS

Nonstick cooking spray, for the pan

Flaky Pie Dough (page 149)

4 large crisp-tart baking apples (about 2 pounds total), such as Honeycrisp, Gala, or Pink Lady

3 tablespoons fresh lemon juice

2 tablespoons unsalted butter

½ cup firmly packed light brown sugar

¼ cup seedless raspberry jam

½ teaspoon pumpkin pie spice

¼ cup store-bought caramel sauce, for drizzling

Lightly spray 12 standard muffin cups with cooking spray. On a lightly floured work surface, roll out the dough into a 12-inch round about ⅛ inch thick. Using a 4-inch round cookie cutter, cut out as many rounds as possible. Gather up the dough scraps, press them together, roll out, and cut out more rounds. You should have 12 rounds total. Transfer each round to a prepared muffin cup, gently pressing the dough evenly onto the bottom and up the sides. The edge of the dough should reach just below rim. Place the lined muffin cups in the refrigerator while you prepare the apples.

Stand an apple, stem end up, on a cutting board. Using a sharp knife, and placing it just to the side of the stem, cut straight down. Rotate the apple 180 degrees and cut down the same way on the opposite side. Cut off the remaining two sides the same way and discard the core. You should have 4 pieces total, 2 large and 2 small. Trim the top and bottom off of each large piece. Using the same sharp knife or a mandoline, cut the larger pieces crosswise into very thin half-moons (about 1⁄16 inch thick). Cut the smaller apple pieces lengthwise into very thin half-moons. Transfer all the slices to a large bowl. Repeat with the remaining apples. Sprinkle the apple slices with the lemon juice and toss gently to coat evenly.

Continued on page 106

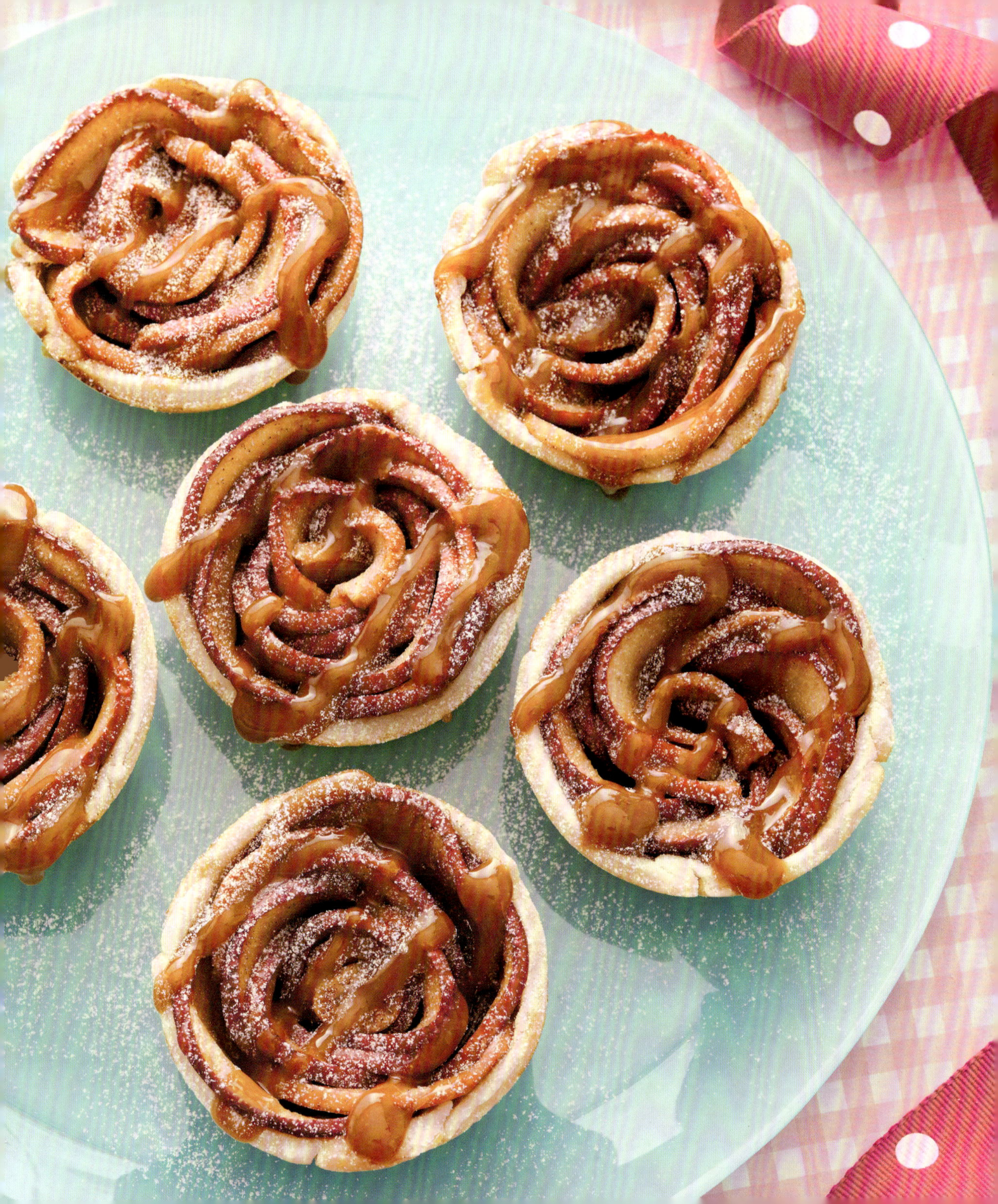

> **Make It Special**
> You can dust the tops of these sweet tartlets with powdered sugar, top with a dainty scoop of ice cream, or garnish with pink rose petals.

~ *Continued from page 104* ~

In a small saucepan over medium-low heat, melt the butter. Add the sugar, jam, and pumpkin pie spice and bring to a gentle boil, stirring constantly to dissolve the sugar, about 2 minutes. Remove from the heat, pour over the apple slices, and stir gently to coat evenly, being careful not to break the slices. Transfer about one-third of the apples to a microwave-safe plate, spread in an even layer, and microwave on high power for 1 minute to make the slices pliable. Transfer to a large rimmed baking sheet. Repeat with the remaining apples in two additions. Spread the apple slices in an even layer on the baking sheet.

Preheat the oven to 375°F. To make each apple rose, arrange about 12 apple slices in a straight line, with each slice overlapping the adjoining slice about halfway. The line of apple slices should be about 12 inches long. Starting at the end at which you laid down the first apple slice, gently roll up the apple slices, doing your best to keep the bottom aligned. Carefully transfer the apple "rose" to the center of a pastry-lined muffin cup. Fill in around the edges of the rose with additional slices. Repeat with the remaining apple slices to fill all the lined muffin cups.

Bake the tartlets until the crust is golden brown and the apples are tender, about 40 minutes. Let cool in the cups on a wire rack for at least 20 minutes, then carefully remove the tartlets from the cups.

Serve the tartlets warm or at room temperature, drizzled with the caramel sauce.

Peach Slab Pie

When you're expecting a crowd for your birthday party, this slab pie is a delicious solution. A half sheet pan is the perfect size to hold sweet, seasonal fruit, and because this is a shallow pie, it is easy to portion out to guests. Swap out the peaches for other fruits, such as sliced apples or blueberries, depending on the season.

MAKES 10–12 SERVINGS

FOR THE DOUGH

5 cups all-purpose flour, plus more for the work surface

3 tablespoons sugar

1½ teaspoons salt

1½ cups (3 sticks) cold unsalted butter, cubed

1½ cups ice-cold water, or more if needed

Nonstick cooking spray, for the pan

FOR THE FILLING

About 6 pounds peaches or nectarines, pitted and sliced

½ cup firmly packed light brown sugar

⅓ cup granulated sugar

¼ cup tapioca flour or cornstarch

2 tablespoons fresh lemon juice

To make the dough, in a food processor, combine the flour, sugar, and salt and pulse a few times to mix. Scatter the butter over the flour mixture and pulse just until the butter is about the size of small peas. Evenly sprinkle the water over the flour mixture, then process just until the mixture starts to come together in a shaggy dough, adding a little more water if the dough crumbles when pinched between fingertips. Turn the dough out onto a lightly floured work surface, bring the dough together in a ball, and divide in half. Press each half into a thick disk. Wrap each disk in plastic wrap and refrigerate for at least 30 minutes or up to 1 day. (The dough can also be frozen for up to 1 month; thaw in the refrigerator before using.)

Spray an 18-by-13-inch baking sheet with 1-inch sides with cooking spray. On a floured work surface, roll out a dough disk into a rectangle 20 by 15 inches and about ⅛ inch thick. Carefully transfer the dough to the prepared baking sheet, centering it in the pan and easing it up the sides. There will be some dough overhang but don't trim it yet. Refrigerate the dough-lined baking sheet.

Preheat the oven to 375°F.

To make the filling, in a large bowl, toss together the peaches, both sugars, the tapioca flour, and the lemon juice, coating the fruit evenly.

Continued on page 109

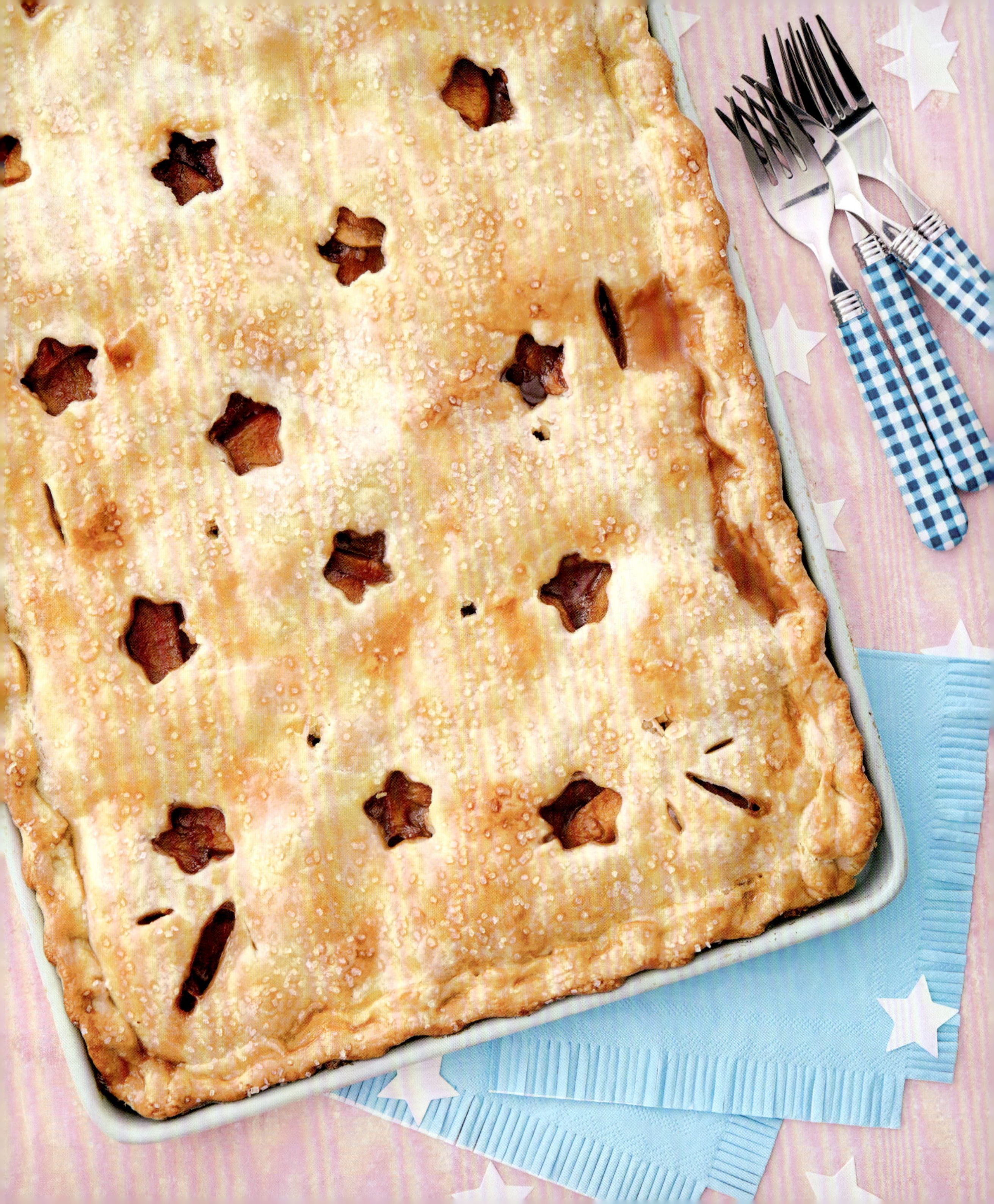

~ Continued from page 107 ~

1 egg beaten with 1 teaspoon cold water, for egg wash

Sparkle sugar, for decorating

On a floured work surface, roll out the second dough disk into a rectangle 18 by 13 inches and about ⅛ inch thick. Trim it to fit the rimmed baking sheet exactly (use a second pan as a template). Using a small cookie or pastry cutter, cut out several evenly spaced small shapes to allow steam to escape.

Spread the peach mixture evenly in the dough-lined baking sheet. Top with the second rectangle of dough. Brush the edge of the top crust with the egg wash. Fold the edge of the bottom crust up and over the top crust to seal, then flute or crimp to finish the edge. Brush the top crust and the edge with the egg wash and sprinkle with sparkle sugar.

Bake the pie until the crust is golden brown and the filling juices are bubbling, about 1 hour. Let cool on a wire rack for at least 1 hour before serving.

Cream Top

For a yummy presentation, top the whole slab pie with scoops of ice cream or dollops of whipped cream before cutting and serving.

Banana Chocolate Cream Pie

With layers of dark chocolate ganache, vanilla-scented custard, and whipped cream, this is the ultimate banana cream pie. Sandwiching the banana slices between the layers of creamy custard keeps them from browning. Choose just-ripe bananas for this dessert.

MAKES 6–8 SERVINGS

Flaky Pie Dough (page 149)

FOR THE GANACHE

3 ounces bittersweet chocolate, chopped

¼ cup heavy cream

1 tablespoon unsalted butter

FOR THE CUSTARD

½ cup sugar

¼ cup cornstarch

¼ teaspoon salt

2 cups whole milk

4 large egg yolks

2 tablespoons unsalted butter

2 teaspoons vanilla extract

2 large, ripe but firm bananas, peeled and sliced

Whipped Cream (page 140)

Prepare the dough and chill as directed. On a lightly floured work surface, roll out the dough into a round about 12 inches in diameter and about ⅛ inch thick. Line a 9-inch pie pan with the dough round. Trim the edge, leaving a 1-inch overhang. Fold the overhang under itself and crimp or flute to create a decorative edge. Refrigerate or freeze until firm, about 30 minutes.

Preheat the oven to 400°F. Line the pie shell with aluminum foil and fill with pie weights. Bake the crust until it starts to look dry, about 15 minutes. Remove the weights and foil and continue baking until golden, about 15 minutes longer. Let cool completely on a wire rack.

To make the ganache, in a small saucepan over low heat, combine the chocolate, cream, and butter and heat, stirring constantly, just until smooth. Pour into a small bowl and let cool until cool to the touch but still spreadable, about 20 minutes. Whisk until smooth, then spread evenly over the bottom of the chilled crust. Set aside.

To make the custard, in a medium saucepan, whisk together the sugar, cornstarch, and salt. Slowly whisk in the milk. Place over medium heat and heat, whisking occasionally, just until small bubbles appear along the edges of the pan. Remove from the heat. In a medium bowl, whisk the egg yolks until blended. Add about one-fourth of the warm milk mixture to the yolks while whisking constantly. Then whisk the egg yolk mixture into the warm milk mixture. Return the pan to medium heat and cook, stirring constantly, until the custard thickens and is smooth and silky, about 7 minutes. Remove from

Block of bittersweet chocolate, at room temperature, for garnish

the heat and stir in the butter and vanilla. Pour through a fine-mesh sieve into a heatproof bowl. Cover with plastic wrap, pressing it directly onto the surface of the custard (to prevent a "skin" from forming). Let cool for 15 minutes.

Uncover the custard and dollop half of it over the chocolate layer in the pie shell, spreading it evenly to the edge of the pie shell without disturbing the chocolate. Arrange the banana slices in an even layer on top of the custard. Dollop the remaining custard over the bananas and spread evenly to the edge of the pie shell. Cover with plastic wrap and refrigerate until well chilled, about 3 hours.

To serve, mound the whipped cream on top of the pie. Then, holding the chocolate block over the pie and using a vegetable peeler, cut thin shavings from the chocolate, distributing them evenly over the top.

Specialty Sweets

Birthday Cake Brownies

Rich chocolate brownies with a cream cheesecake filling make perfect individual treats for a birthday fete any time of year. Top with ice cream—vanilla or your favorite flavor—and finish with plenty of colorful sprinkles, if you like.

MAKES 9 BROWNIES

FOR THE BROWNIES

½ cup unsalted butter, plus more for the pan

4 ounces unsweetened chocolate, finely chopped

1 cup all-purpose flour

¼ teaspoon salt

3 large eggs

1¾ cups sugar

1 teaspoon vanilla extract

FOR THE CHEESECAKE FILLING

6 ounces cream cheese, at room temperature

¼ cup sugar

1 large egg

1 teaspoon vanilla extract

¼ cup rainbow sprinkles

Vanilla ice cream, for serving

Preheat the oven to 325°F. Butter a 9-inch square baking pan, then press a piece of parchment paper across the bottom and up over two sides of the pan, leaving a 2-inch overhang on both sides. Butter the parchment.

To make the the brownies batter, fill a medium saucepan one-third full with water and heat until barely simmering over medium-low heat. Rest a heatproof bowl in the rim of the saucepan over (not touching) the water, add the butter and chocolate, and heat, stirring often, until the butter and chocolate have melted and the mixture is smooth, 3–4 minutes. Turn off the heat, remove the bowl, and let the chocolate mixture cool slightly.

In a small bowl, sift together the flour and salt. In a large bowl, whisk together the eggs and sugar until blended and smooth. Add the chocolate mixture and vanilla and whisk until mixed. Whisk in the dry ingredients until incorporated.

To make the cheesecake filling, in a bowl, stir together the cream cheese, sugar, egg, and vanilla until smooth and creamy. Add the sprinkles and stir to mix evenly.

Pour two-thirds of the batter into the prepared pan. Spoon the cheesecake filling over the batter. Dollop the remaining batter over the cheesecake filling. Starting in one corner, swirl a spoon through the layers to create a marbled pattern. Starting from another corner, repeat the swirling.

Bake the brownies until a toothpick inserted into the center comes out with moist crumbs attached, 35–40 minutes. Let cool on a wire rack to room temperature. Use the parchment overhang to lift the brownies from the pan and transfer to a cutting board. Cut into squares and serve with ice cream.

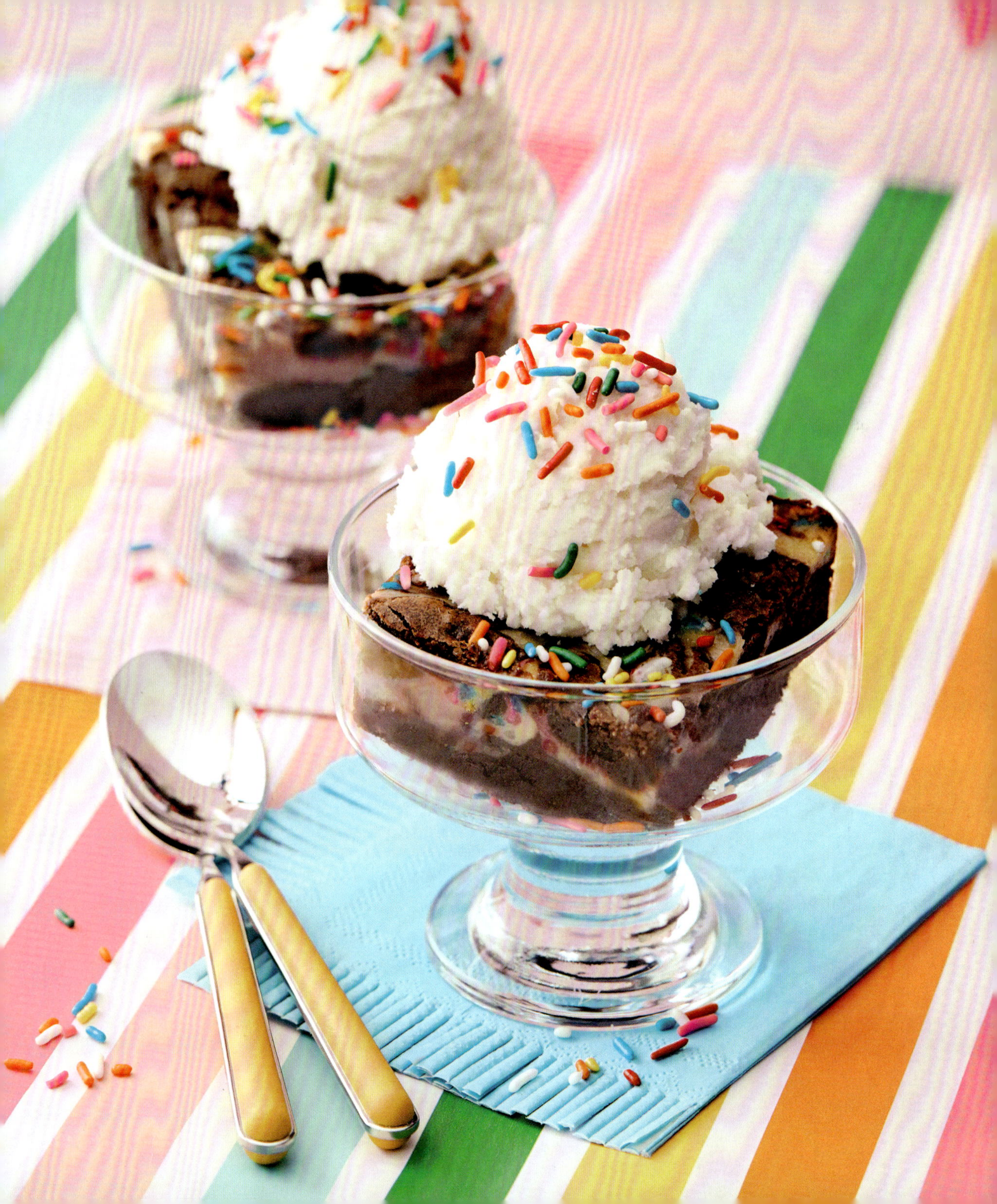

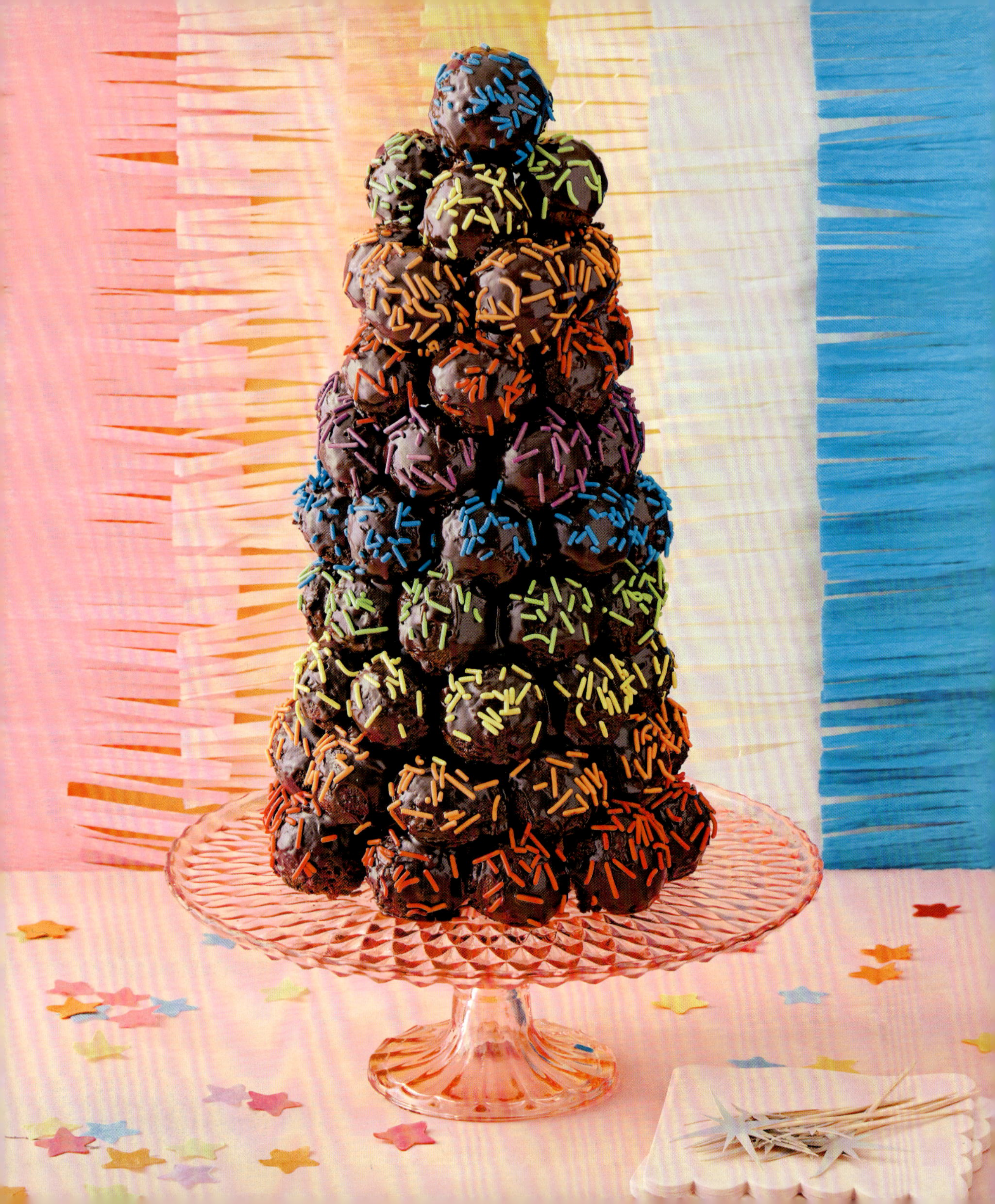

Chocolate-Glazed Doughnut Hole Cone Cake

This festive doughnut tower will shine at the center of any party table. The rustic chocolate doughnut holes are yummy all by themselves, but layered onto a cone, they are both fun to look at and fun to eat. Edible flowers or candies hide any gaps in your tower. In a pinch, you can purchase the holes from a local doughnut shop.

MAKES ABOUT 45 DONUT HOLES

FOR THE DOUGHNUT HOLES

- 1½ cups all-purpose flour
- 1½ cups cake flour
- ½ cup unsweetened natural cocoa powder
- 1½ teaspoons baking powder
- ¾ teaspoon baking soda
- ¾ teaspoon salt
- 3 large eggs
- ¾ cup sugar
- ¾ cup buttermilk
- 3 tablespoons unsalted butter, melted
- 2 teaspoons vanilla extract
- Canola or peanut oil, for deep-frying

To make the doughnut holes, in a medium bowl, sift together both flours, the cocoa powder, baking powder, baking soda, and salt. In a large bowl, using an electric mixer, beat together the eggs and sugar on medium speed until creamy and pale, about 3 minutes. Add the buttermilk, melted butter, and vanilla and beat until blended. On low speed, add the flour mixture and beat until the mixture comes together in a soft dough.

Line a rimmed baking sheet with paper towels and set it near the stove. Pour oil to a depth of 1½ to 2 inches into a deep, heavy frying pan or sauté pan (no more than half full) and heat over medium-high heat to 360°F on a deep-frying thermometer.

Working in batches of about 6 doughnut holes at a time, drop the dough by tablespoonfuls (a small cookie scoop works well for this) into the hot oil and deep-fry, using a slotted spoon to turn the holes a few times, until golden and cooked through, about 3 minutes. Using the slotted spoon, transfer the holes to the towel-lined pan. Repeat with the remaining dough, always allowing the oil to return to 360°F between batches.

Continued on page 118

~ Continued from page 117 ~

Chocolate Glaze (page 144) or Vanilla Glaze (page 144)

About 1 cup rainbow or other sprinkles, for decorating

FOR THE CONE

12-inch-tall Styrofoam cone, wrapped with aluminum foil

About 45 toothpicks

Edible flowers, for decorating (optional)

Place a large wire rack on top of a sheet of parchment paper. Have the glaze ready in a small bowl. When the doughnut holes are cool enough to handle, one at a time, dip them into the glaze, letting any excess drip back into the bowl, and place on the wire rack. While the glaze is still wet, scatter the sprinkles over the doughnut holes. Let stand until the glaze sets slightly, about 10 minutes.

To assemble the cone cake, starting at the base of the cone and placing them as closely together as possible, insert a toothpick through each doughnut hole and attach it to the cone, working upward in rows of doughnut holes. You can leave the end of the toothpick sticking out until finished. If you like, especially toward the top of the cone, cut a thin slice from the base of each doughnut hole to help the shape taper properly. Finish with a doughnut hole attached to the top of the cone. Using a thimble, push the toothpicks into the doughnut holes until they are no longer visible.

If you like, decorate the cone by pushing edible flowers into any gaps between the doughnut holes. Serve right away. The doughnut holes taste best the day they are made.

Strawberries and Cream Puffs

Here, purchased puff pastry is baked until golden and crisp and then used to sandwich a filling of sugared strawberries and whipped cream, a showy yet dessert guaranteed to please. If you like, use whole raspberries or sliced blackberries in place of the strawberries.

MAKES 6 SERVINGS

2 sheets frozen puff pastry (about 1 pound), thawed according to package instructions

All-purpose flour, for the work surface

1½ cups hulled and thinly sliced strawberries

Juice of ½ lemon

3 tablespoons granulated sugar

1½ cups cold heavy cream

1 teaspoon vanilla extract

6 Strawberry "Roses" (page 146) or small strawberries, for garnish

Powdered sugar, for dusting

Line a large rimmed baking sheet with parchment paper. Lay 1 puff pastry sheet on a lightly floured work surface and roll it out in to a rectangle 8 by 6 inches and about ⅛ inch thick. Use a pastry cutter or sharp knife to cut the pastry sheet in half so you have two rectangles that are 4 by 6 inches each, then cut each half crosswise into 3 equal rectangles that measure 4 by 2 inches; you should have 6 rectangles. Repeat with the second pastry sheet. Transfer the 12 rectangles to the prepared baking sheet, spacing them about ½ inch apart. Prick each rectangle four times with a fork. Refrigerate for about 30 minutes.

Preheat the oven to 400°F. Bake the pastry until it is puffed and golden, about 20 minutes. Let cool completely on the pan on a wire rack.

Meanwhile, in a large bowl, combine the strawberries, lemon juice, and 1 tablespoon of the granulated sugar and stir to coat evenly.

In a medium bowl, using an electric mixer, beat together the cream, the remaining 2 tablespoons granulated sugar, and the vanilla on medium-high speed until medium-stiff peaks form. Gently fold about two-thirds of the whipped cream into the strawberry mixture. Transfer the remaining whipped cream to a piping bag fitted with a large open star tip.

To serve, top half of the pastry rectangles with the strawberry-cream mixture, dividing it evenly. Top each with one of the remaining pastry rectangles. Pipe whipped cream on top, then garnish each puff with a strawberry. Using a fine-mesh sieve, dust with powdered sugar.

Cinnamon-Sugar Churros with Chocolate Sauce

Churros—long strips of deep-fried dough popular in Spain and Portugal—are made from choux pastry, the same dough used for making profiteroles (page 81). The dough keeps them light and airy—perfect for sprinkling with cinnamon sugar and dipping into rich chocolate sauce.

MAKES 6 SERVINGS

1 cup water

¼ teaspoon salt

3 tablespoons sugar

1 cup all-purpose flour, sifted

2 large eggs, beaten

Peanut or canola oil, for deep-frying

1 tablespoon ground cinnamon

Chocolate Sauce (page 145), warmed

In a medium saucepan over high heat, combine the water, salt, and 1 tablespoon of the sugar and bring to a boil. Remove from the heat and immediately add the flour. Stir with a wooden spoon until the dough is very smooth and pulls away from the sides of the pan, about 2 minutes. Let cool for 5 minutes, then, using an electric mixer on medium speed, beat in the eggs about 1 tablespoon at a time, beating after each addition until incorporated. Spoon the dough into a piping bag fitted with a large open star tip.

Line a rimmed baking sheet with paper towels and set it near the stove. Pour oil to a depth of 1 inch into a deep, heavy frying pan or sauté pan and heat over medium-high heat to 350°F on a deep-frying thermometer.

Pipe a strip of dough, 3–4 inches long, into the hot oil, using a small knife to cut it free of the piping tip. Pipe several more strips into the pan, being careful not to crowd them and dipping the knife in oil before freeing each strip. Fry the churros, using tongs to turn them as needed, until golden brown and crisp, 3–5 minutes. Using the tongs, transfer the churros to the towel-lined pan to drain briefly, then place them in a large bowl. Repeat with the remaining dough, always allowing the oil to return to 350°F between batches.

In a small bowl, stir together the cinnamon and the remaining 2 tablespoons sugar. Sprinkle over the churros and toss to coat evenly. Serve right away with the warm chocolate sauce alongside for dipping.

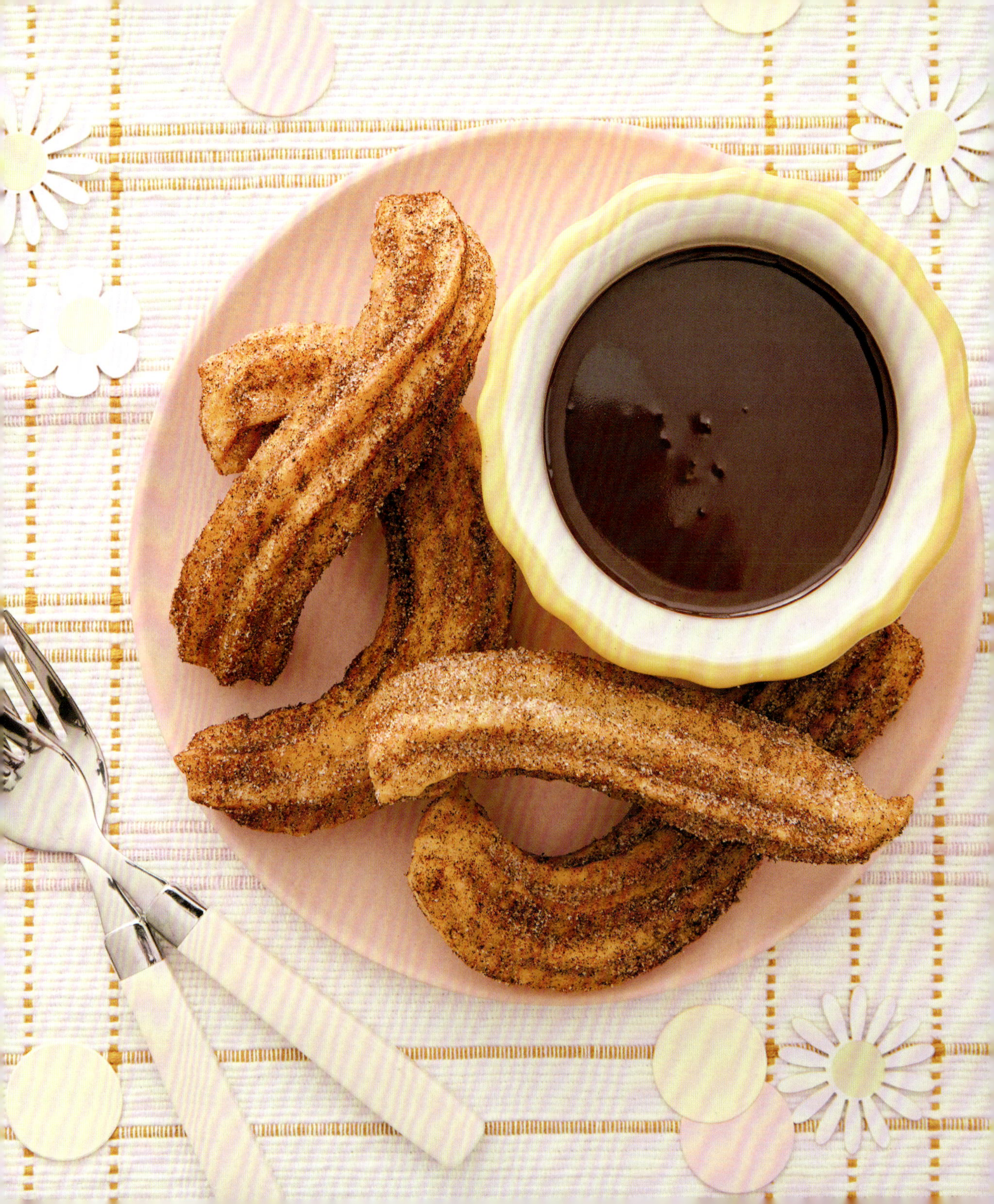

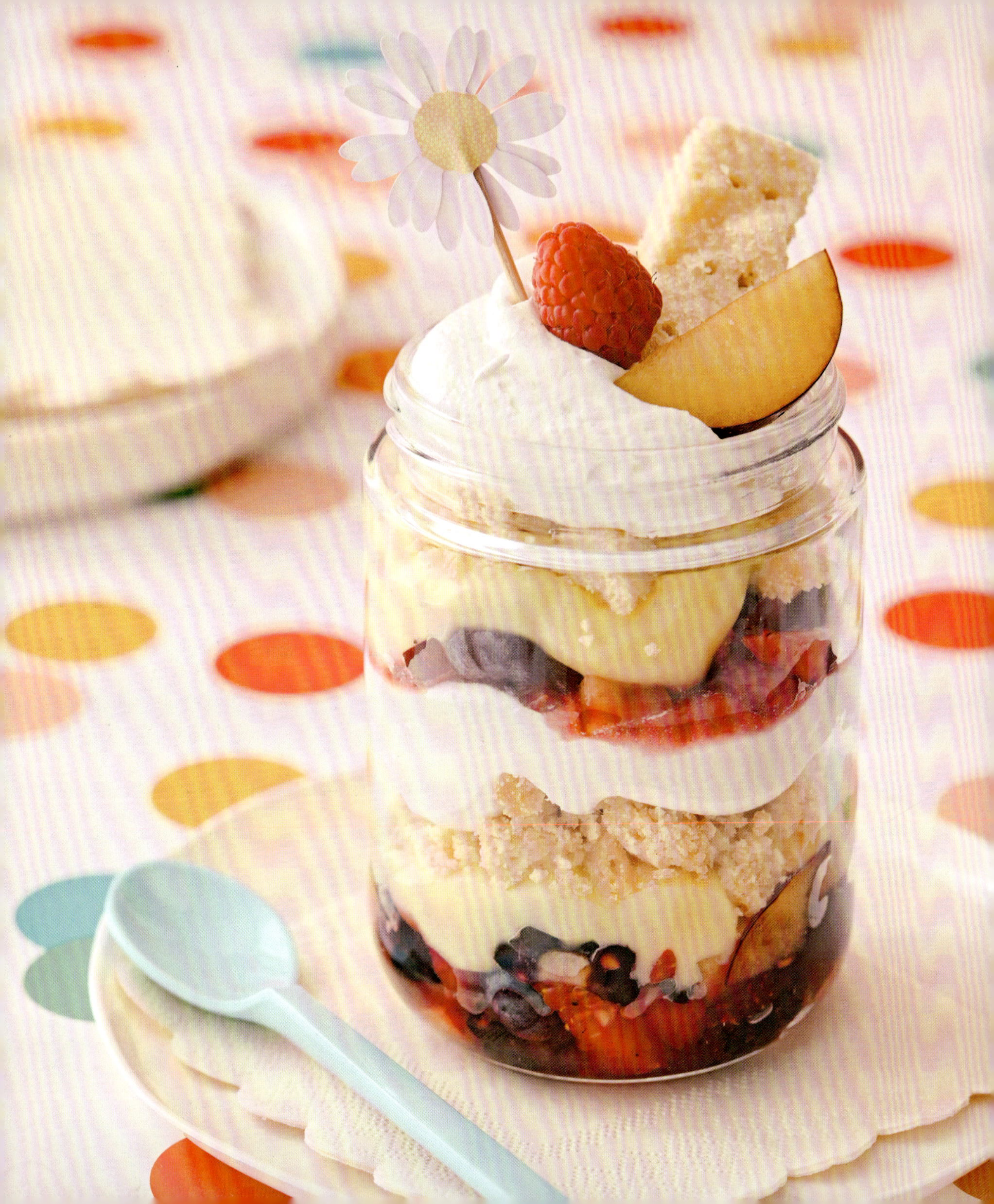

Fruit and Cream Parfaits with Vanilla Shortbread

Layers of fresh fruit, vanilla custard, whipped cream, and your favorite fruit make these parfaits irresistible. The shortbread is amazing on its own, but if you don't have time to make it, use a good-quality purchased shortbread. To transform these parfaits into individual trifles, swap out the shortbread for a few unfrosted vanilla cupcakes.

~ MAKES 6 PARFAITS ~

FOR THE CUSTARD

1¼ cups whole milk

½ cup heavy cream

3 large egg yolks

¼ cup granulated sugar

Pinch of salt

2 tablespoons cornstarch mixed with 1 tablespoon cold water

2 teaspoons vanilla extract

FOR THE SHORTBREAD

1 cup (2 sticks) unsalted butter, at cool room temperature

¼ cup powdered sugar

¼ cup granulated sugar, plus 1 tablespoon for sprinkling

2 teaspoons vanilla extract

1½ cups all-purpose flour

¼ teaspoon salt

To make the custard, in a medium saucepan over low heat, combine the milk and cream and heat until small bubbles appear along the edges of the pan. Remove from the heat. In a medium bowl, whisk together the egg yolks, sugar, and salt until blended, then stir in the cornstarch mixture. Slowly pour about half of the warm milk mixture into the yolk mixture while whisking constantly. Then whisk the egg yolk mixture into the warm milk mixture. Return the pan to medium heat and cook, stirring constantly, until the custard thickens and is smooth and silky, 8–10 minutes. Remove from the heat and stir in the vanilla. Pour through a fine-mesh sieve into a heatproof bowl. Cover with plastic wrap, pressing it directly onto the surface of the custard (to prevent a "skin" from forming), and poke a few holes in the plastic to allow steam to escape. Let cool for several minutes, then refrigerate until chilled, about 2 hours.

To make the shortbread, preheat the oven to 300°F. Have ready an ungreased 9-inch square baking pan.

In a bowl, using an electric mixer, beat the butter on high speed until fluffy. Add the powdered sugar and the ¼ cup granulated sugar and beat on medium speed until the mixture is well blended. Add the vanilla and beat until incorporated. Sift together the flour and salt over the butter mixture and beat on low speed just until blended. Stop the mixer and scrape down the bowl with a rubber spatula, then beat again on low speed just until blended.

~ *Continued on page 124* ~

~ *Continued from page 123* ~

3 cups mixed finely chopped fresh fruit, such as berries, nectarines, peaches, and/or plums, plus 6–12 pieces fruit for garnish

3 tablespoons granulated sugar

3 cups Whipped Cream (page 140)

Transfer the dough to the pan and, using floured fingertips, press the dough into an even layer on the bottom. If you like, smooth it with the flat bottom of a glass. Sprinkle evenly with the remaining 1 tablespoon granulated sugar. Bake the shortbread until the edges are golden, about 1 hour.

Transfer the pan to a wire rack and immediately use a thin, sharp knife to cut the shortbread into 16 bars. With a toothpick or a fork, decorate the shortbread with a pattern of dots. Let cool in the pan on the rack for 30 minutes, then transfer the shortbread to the rack and let cool completely.

When you are ready to assemble the parfaits, in a bowl, stir together the fruit and granulated sugar. Set aside for 15 minutes. Set aside 6 shortbread bars for garnish and roughly crumble the remaining shortbread into a bowl.

Select 6 glasses, each with about 1½-cup capacity. In each glass, layer ¼ cup of the fruit mixture, 2 heaping tablespoons of the custard, a layer of crumbled shortbread, and about 3 tablespoons whipped cream. Repeat the layers of fruit, custard, and crumbled shortbread and then top with the remaining whipped cream. Garnish with a piece of fruit or two and whole shortbread and serve at once.

Raspberry-Swirled Pavlovas

A pavlova is just a fancy name for meringue that is baked into a thick-walled bowl shape and then filled with whipped cream and fruit. To make these little meringue cups extra special, spoon a thin layer of Lemon Curd (page 145) into each one before adding the cream and fruit.

MAKES 6–8 SERVINGS

FOR THE MERINGUES

10 ounces frozen raspberries

2 tablespoons plus 1 cup sugar

4 large egg whites

½ teaspoon cream of tartar

¼ teaspoon salt

FOR THE TOPPING

Whipped Cream (page 140)

About 2 cups fresh raspberries

Small fresh mint sprigs, for garnish (optional)

To make the meringues, preheat the oven to 325°F. Line the bottoms of 2 rimmed baking sheets with parchment paper.

In a blender, combine the frozen raspberries and 2 tablespoons of the sugar and process until a smooth purée forms, stopping the blender to scrape down the sides with a rubber spatula as needed. Pour the purée through a fine-mesh sieve into a small bowl. Using the back of a spoon or a rubber spatula, press against the purée, forcing as much liquid through the sieve as possible. Discard any seeds in the sieve.

In a large bowl, using an electric mixer, beat the egg whites on medium speed until foamy, about 1 minute. Add the cream of tartar and salt and continue to beat on medium speed until the whites begin to thicken, about 2 minutes. Increase the speed to high, slowly sprinkle in the remaining 1 cup sugar, and continue beating until the egg whites hold stiff, glossy peaks, 5–7 minutes.

Stop the mixer and use a rubber spatula to gently fold ⅓ cup of the raspberry purée into the meringue until lightly swirled. Spoon 6–8 mounds of the meringue onto the prepared baking sheet, dividing the meringue evenly and spacing the mounds 1–2 inches apart. Then spoon ½–1 teaspoon raspberry purée on top of each meringue and swirl with a toothpick; reserve the remaining purée. Using the back of a large spoon, create an indentation in the center of each mound and a rim around the edges.

Continued on page 126

Pretty in Pink

To play up the palette, serve these pavlovas with pretty glasses filled with pink lemonade or sparkling water with fresh raspberries.

~ *Continued from page 125* ~

Bake the meringues until the edges are just beginning to set, about 5 minutes. Reduce the oven temperature to 250°F and continue to bake until the meringues are firm and just beginning to brown, about 1 hour longer. Turn off the oven, leave the oven door ajar, and let the meringues cool completely in the oven, about 2 hours.

When ready to serve, arrange the meringues on individual plates. Spoon a big dollop of whipped cream into the hollow in each meringue and top the cream with some fresh raspberries. Drizzle the remaining raspberry purée over the top and garnish each serving with a mint sprig, if using. Serve right away.

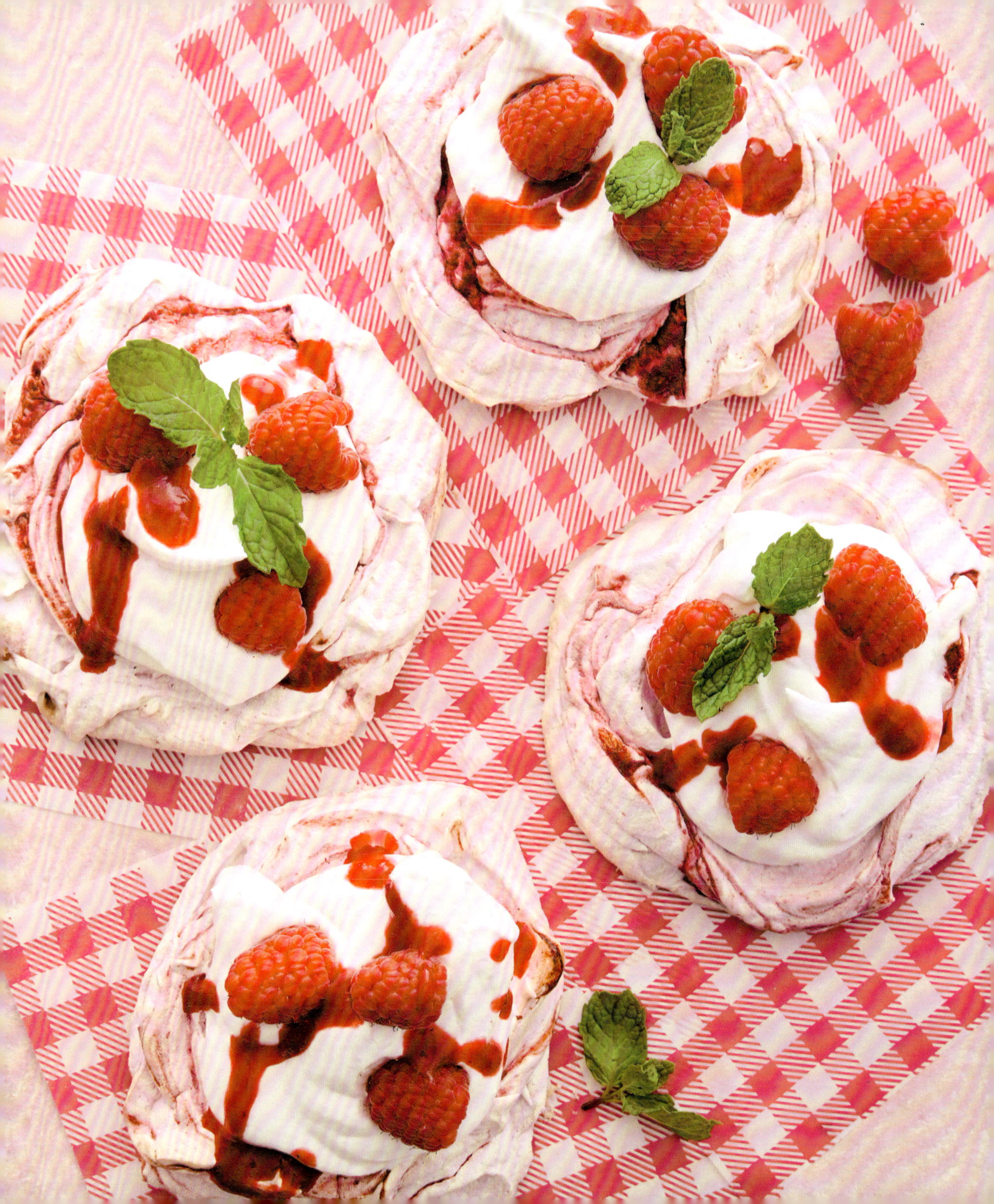

Millionaire's Shortbread

Almost like a homemade candy bar, these cookies, layered with creamy caramel and dark chocolate, take plain shortbread to a new level of stardom. They take a bit of time to make, but they can be prepared a day in advance.

MAKES 9 SHORTBREAD SQUARES

FOR THE CRUST

½ cup cold unsalted butter, cut into cubes, plus more at room temperature for the baking dish

1 cup all-purpose flour

¼ cup firmly packed dark brown sugar

2½ teaspoons cornstarch

½ teaspoon salt

2 tablespoons water

1 large egg yolk

FOR THE CARAMEL

1 can (14 ounces) sweetened condensed milk

½ cup plus 2 tablespoons firmly packed dark brown sugar

7 tablespoons unsalted butter, cut into tablespoon-size pieces

2 tablespoons light corn syrup

To make the crust, preheat the oven to 350°F. Line a 9-inch square baking dish with aluminum foil, pushing it neatly into the corners and letting the foil overhang the sides by about 2 inches on two opposite sides. Repeat with a second piece of foil perpendicular to the first piece so it overhangs the other two sides by about 2 inches. Butter the foil.

In a food processor, combine the flour, brown sugar, cornstarch, and salt and pulse until blended. Scatter the butter evenly over the flour mixture and process until the mixture resembles coarse sand. Add the water and egg yolk and process until moist clumps form and the dough just begins to come together.

Transfer the dough to the prepared pan and press evenly onto the bottom. Pierce the dough all over with a fork and bake until golden brown, about 20 minutes. Transfer the baking dish to a wire rack and let the crust cool slightly.

To make the caramel, in a medium saucepan, whisk together the condensed milk and brown sugar until the sugar dissolves. Add the butter, corn syrup, vanilla, and salt, place over medium heat, and bring to a gentle boil, stirring often with a whisk. Then cook, whisking constantly, until the mixture darkens slightly, thickens, and registers 220°F on a candy thermometer, 7–10 minutes. If the caramel begins to scorch, reduce the heat. Carefully pour the caramel over the warm crust and let cool until set, about 20 minutes.

1½ teaspoons vanilla extract

½ teaspoon salt

FOR THE CHOCOLATE TOPPING

1½ cups semisweet chocolate chips

¼ cup heavy cream

Flaky sea salt, for sprinkling (optional)

To make the chocolate topping, in a small microwave-safe bowl, combine the chocolate and cream. Microwave on high power, stopping and stirring every 30 seconds, until the chocolate is almost completely melted, then stir until smooth. Pour the chocolate over the set caramel, spread in an even layer, and let cool slightly. Sprinkle sea salt over the chocolate, if desired. Cover the baking dish with plastic wrap and refrigerate the dessert until firm, at least 2 hours or up to overnight.

Use the foil overhang to lift the dessert from the baking dish and transfer it to a cutting board. Cut into squares to serve.

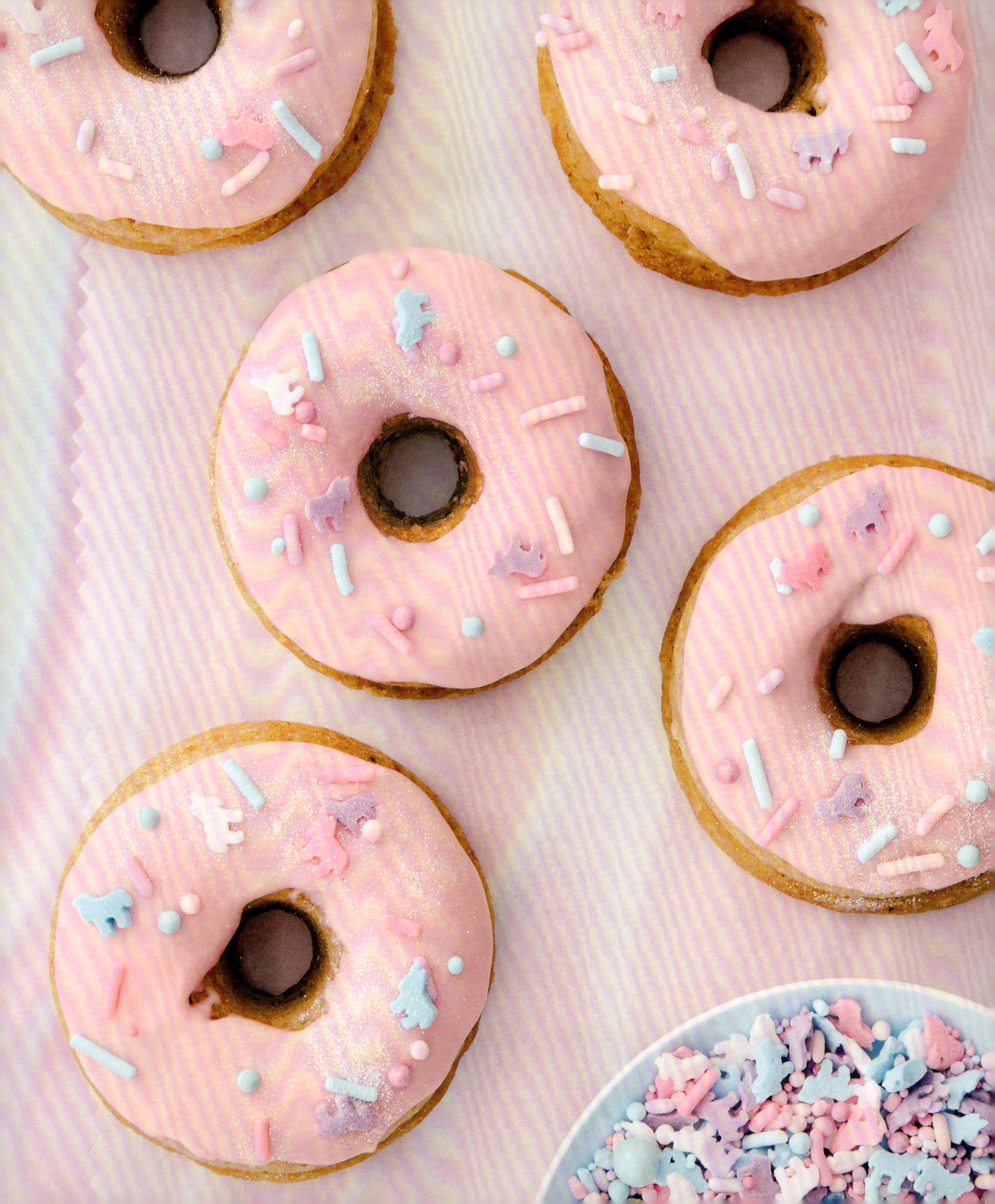

Unicorn Rainbow Doughnuts

These cakey, tender vanilla doughnuts are easy to make because they are baked, plus a doughnut pan makes quick work of shaping them. Choose food coloring in your favorite color to tint the Vanilla Glaze, and then pull out your fanciest sprinkles and edible glitter to create showstopping toppings.

MAKES 9 DOUGHNUTS

FOR THE DOUGHNUTS

Nonstick cooking spray, for the pans

1½ cups all-purpose flour

1 teaspoon baking powder

¼ teaspoon baking soda

¼ teaspoon salt

¼ teaspoon freshly grated nutmeg

¼ cup granulated sugar

¼ cup firmly packed light brown sugar

2 tablespoons unsalted butter, at room temperature

2 tablespoons canola oil

1 large egg

½ cup buttermilk

1 tablespoon vanilla extract

FOR DECORATING

Vanilla Glaze (page 144)

Pastel gel food coloring

Sprinkles and edible glitter

To make the doughnuts, preheat the oven to 375°F. Spray two 6-cup doughnut pans with cooking spray.

In a medium bowl, whisk together the flour, baking powder, baking soda, salt, and nutmeg. In a large bowl, using an electric mixer, beat together both sugars, the butter, and the oil on medium speed until well blended and smooth. Add the egg and beat until incorporated, then beat in the buttermilk and vanilla until well blended and smooth. Stop the mixer and scrape down the bowl with a rubber spatula. On low speed, add the flour mixture and beat just until blended. The batter will be thick.

Spoon the batter into a piping bag fitted with a large round tip and pipe into 9 of the prepared doughnut cups, dividing it evenly. Bake the doughnuts until the edges are golden, about 10 minutes. Turn out the doughnuts onto a wire rack and let cool slightly.

While the doughnuts are baking, make the vanilla glaze and tint it light purple or pink—or another favorite pastel—with the food coloring.

While the doughnuts are still warm, working with one at a time, dip the top of each doughnut into the glaze, then return the doughnut, top side up, to the rack. Immediately, while the glaze is still wet, decorate the doughnuts with the sprinkles and edible glitter. Let stand until the glaze is set, about 10 minutes, before serving.

Chocolate Mousse Cups

A tablespoon of instant coffee powder added to chocolate heightens the flavor of the chocolate, but if coffee is not your thing, you can leave it out. Top each serving with swirls of whipped cream, which help cut the richness, and your favorite crunchy cookie, which adds a little texture.

MAKES 6 SERVINGS

10 ounces semisweet chocolate, finely chopped

1½ cups cold heavy cream

⅔ cup powdered sugar

1 tablespoon instant coffee powder

1 teaspoon vanilla extract

Whipped Cream (page 140)

Chocolate or rainbow sprinkles, for decorating

6 chocolate wafer cookies, for garnish (optional)

Fill a medium saucepan one-third full with water and heat until barely simmering over medium-low heat. Rest a heatproof bowl in the rim of the saucepan over (not touching) the water, add the chocolate, and heat, stirring often, just until melted. Turn off the heat, remove the bowl, and stir the chocolate until smooth. Let the chocolate cool until cool to the touch but still pourable, about 30 minutes.

In a medium bowl, using an electric mixer, beat together the cream, powdered sugar, coffee powder, and vanilla on medium-high speed until medium-firm peaks form. Whisk about one-third of the whipped cream into the cooled chocolate until smooth. Using a rubber spatula, fold the remaining whipped cream into the chocolate mixture just until no white streaks are visible.

Divide the mousse evenly among 6 individual bowls. Cover and refrigerate for at least 2 hours or up to overnight.

To serve, top each serving with the whipped cream and decorate the cream with sprinkles. Garnish each serving with a cookie, if using, and serve right away.

Rainbow Rice Crispy Pops

Puffed rice cereal and marshmallow squares are always welcome at a party. But dipped in colorful candy coating and sprinkles, these old-fashioned treats become a work of edible art. Enclosed in cellophane bags and tied with a ribbon, they make great party favors.

MAKES ABOUT 25 POPS

3 tablespoons unsalted butter, plus more at room temperature for the waxed paper

4 cups miniature marshmallows

6 cups crisped rice cereal

1 bag (12 ounces) pale pink, yellow, or blue candy melts (2 cups)

Rainbow sprinkles, for decorating

Place a large sheet of waxed paper on a work surface and butter the paper.

In a medium saucepan over low heat, melt the butter. Add the marshmallows and stir until completely melted. Add the cereal and stir until evenly coated. Remove from the heat and let cool slightly, then dump the cereal mixture onto the prepared waxed paper. Moisten your hands with water and spread the mixture into a rectangle about 10 by 15 inches. Let cool completely.

Using a long knife, cut the cereal block into rectangles about 2 by 3 inches. Working from a narrow end, insert a wooden ice-pop stick halfway into each rectangle, leaving the other half sticking out to use for holding the pop. You should have about 25 pops.

Fill a medium saucepan one-third full with water and heat until barely simmering over medium-low heat. Rest a heatproof bowl in the rim of the saucepan over (not touching) the water, add the candy melts, and heat, stirring often, just until melted and smooth, 5–7 minutes. Remove the pan from the heat. Leave the bowl atop the pan to keep warm.

Pour the sprinkles into a small, shallow bowl. Line the bottoms of 2 rimmed baking sheets with waxed paper. Carefully dip and swirl each pop in the melted candy and then dip into the sprinkles. As each pop is coated, place it on a prepared pan. Refrigerate for 10 minutes to set the coating before serving.

Basic Recipes

Vanilla Frosting

MAKES ABOUT 4 CUPS

1 cup unsalted butter, at cool room temperature

5 cups powdered sugar

¼ cup heavy cream or whole milk

1 tablespoon vanilla extract

Pinch of salt

In a large bowl, using an electric mixer, beat the butter on medium-high speed until pale and fluffy, about 1 minute. Stop the mixer. Sift half of the sugar into the bowl and mix on low speed just until blended. Stop the mixer. Sift the remaining sugar into the bowl and add the cream, vanilla, and salt. Mix on low speed just until blended. Stop the mixer and scrape down the bowl with a rubber spatula. Beat on medium-high speed until the frosting is airy and smooth, about 5 minutes.

Variation

Mint Frosting: Make ½ recipe Vanilla Frosting, omitting the vanilla extract and adding ½ teaspoon peppermint extract and a few drops of green gel food coloring.

Cookies and Cream Frosting: Make the frosting as directed. Stir 1 cup finely ground chocolate sandwich cookies into the finished frosting.

Cookie Dough Frosting: Make ½ recipe Vanilla Frosting. Add ⅓ cup edible cookie dough (page 57) to the finished frosting and beat until well blended.

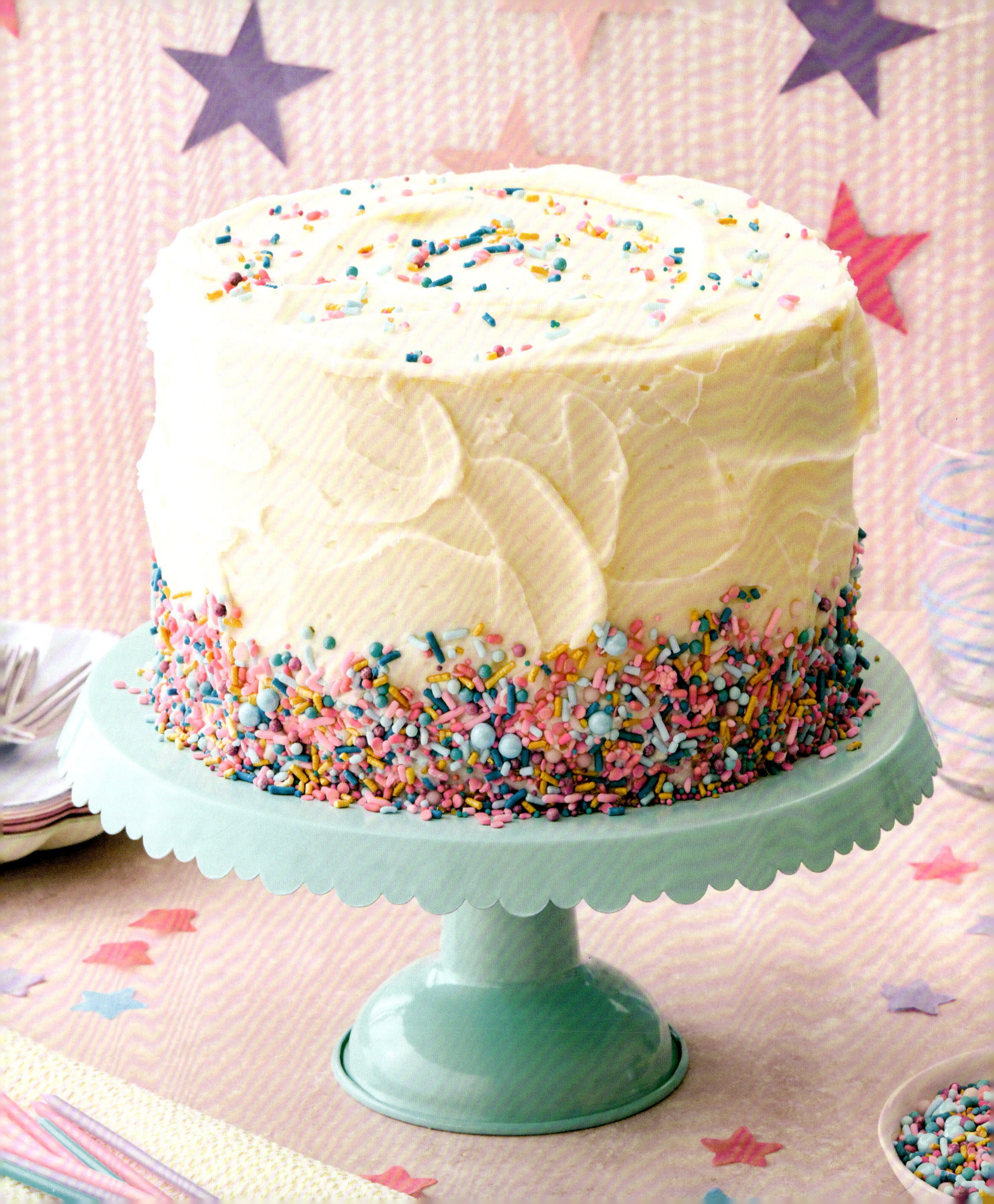

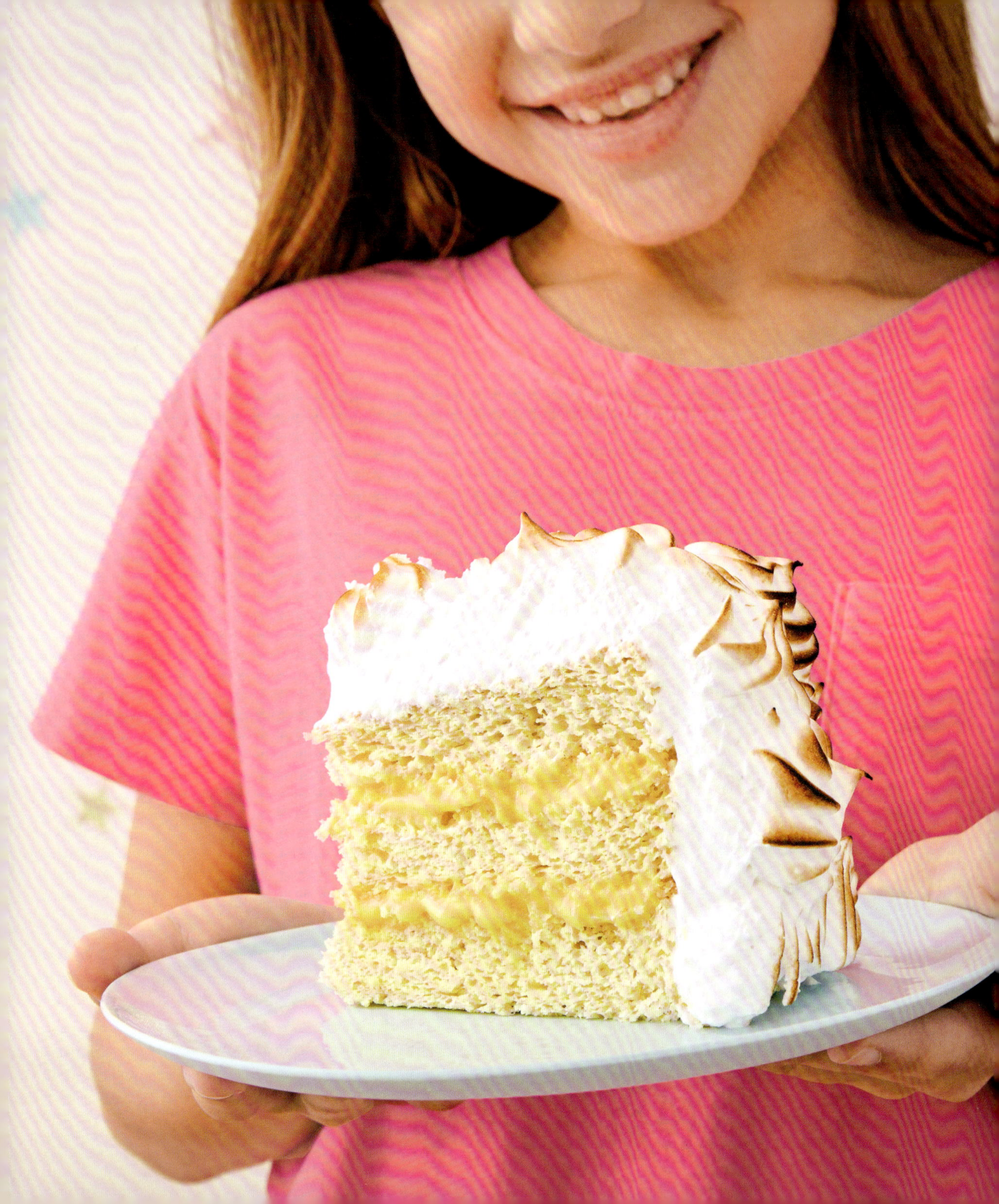

Meringue Frosting

MAKES ENOUGH FOR ONE 8- OR 9-INCH ROUND LAYER CAKE

1⅓ cups plus 2 tablespoons sugar

¼ teaspoon salt

½ cup water

6 large egg whites

½ teaspoon cream of tartar

1 teaspoon vanilla extract

First make a sugar syrup. In a medium saucepan, combine 1⅓ cups of the sugar, the salt, and the water and stir to moisten the sugar evenly. Place over medium heat and bring to a boil, stirring to dissolve the sugar. Once the mixture begins to bubble, increase the heat to medium-high and cook, without stirring, until the sugar syrup registers 240°F on a candy thermometer. If sugar crystals form on the sides of the pan, wash them down with a pastry brush dipped in cold water.

While the syrup is cooking, in a stand mixer fitted with the whisk attachment, beat together the egg whites and cream of tartar on medium speed until the mixture is foamy. Slowly add the remaining 2 tablespoons sugar, increase the speed to medium-high, and beat until medium-firm peaks form. Reduce the speed to medium and slowly pour in the hot syrup in a thin stream, aiming it away from the beater and close to the side of the bowl, until all the syrup is incorporated. Then increase the speed to high and beat until a thick, glossy meringue forms, about 4 minutes. Add the vanilla and beat for 1 minute. Use right away.

Cream Cheese Frosting

MAKES ENOUGH FOR ONE 9-INCH LAYER CAKE, 12 STANDARD CUPCAKES, OR 24 MINI CUPCAKES

12 ounces cream cheese, at room temperature

6 tablespoons (¾ stick) unsalted butter, at room temperature

2 teaspoons vanilla extract

1½ cups powdered sugar, sifted

In a stand mixer fitted with the paddle attachment, beat together the cream cheese, butter, and vanilla on medium-high speed until light and fluffy, about 2 minutes. Gradually beat in the sugar and then continue to beat until thoroughly combined, stopping the mixer to scrape down the bowl with a rubber spatula as needed. If the consistency is too soft, refrigerate the frosting until it is spreadable, about 15 minutes. The frosting will keep in an airtight container in the refrigerator for up to 3 days.

Whipped Cream

MAKES ABOUT 2 CUPS

1 cup cold heavy cream

1 tablespoon sugar

½ teaspoon vanilla extract

If you have time, chill the bowl and the beater in the refrigerator or freezer for about 30 minutes. In the bowl, using an an electric mixer, beat together the cream, sugar and vanilla on medium-high speed until medium-stiff peaks form, 3–4 minutes.

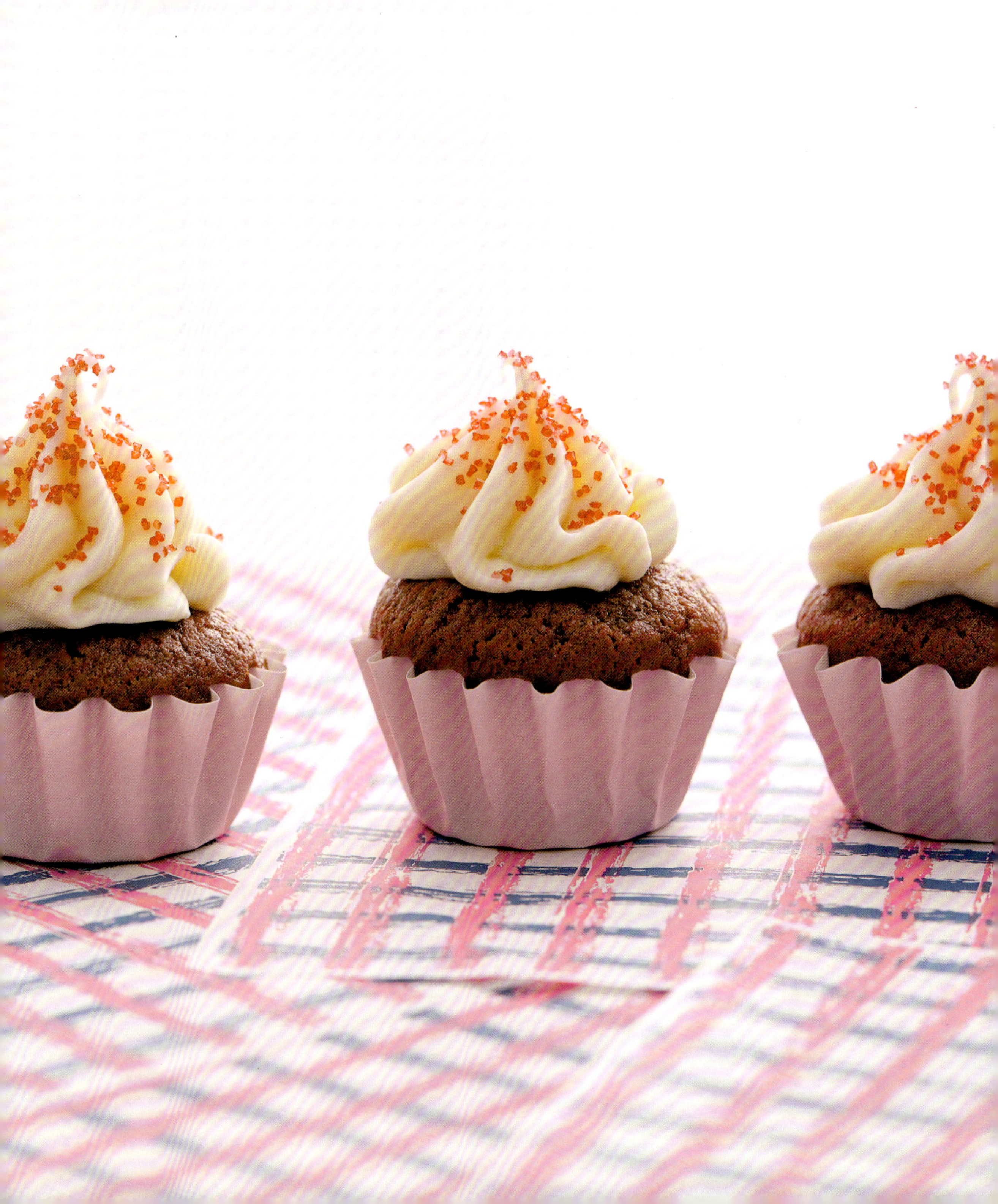

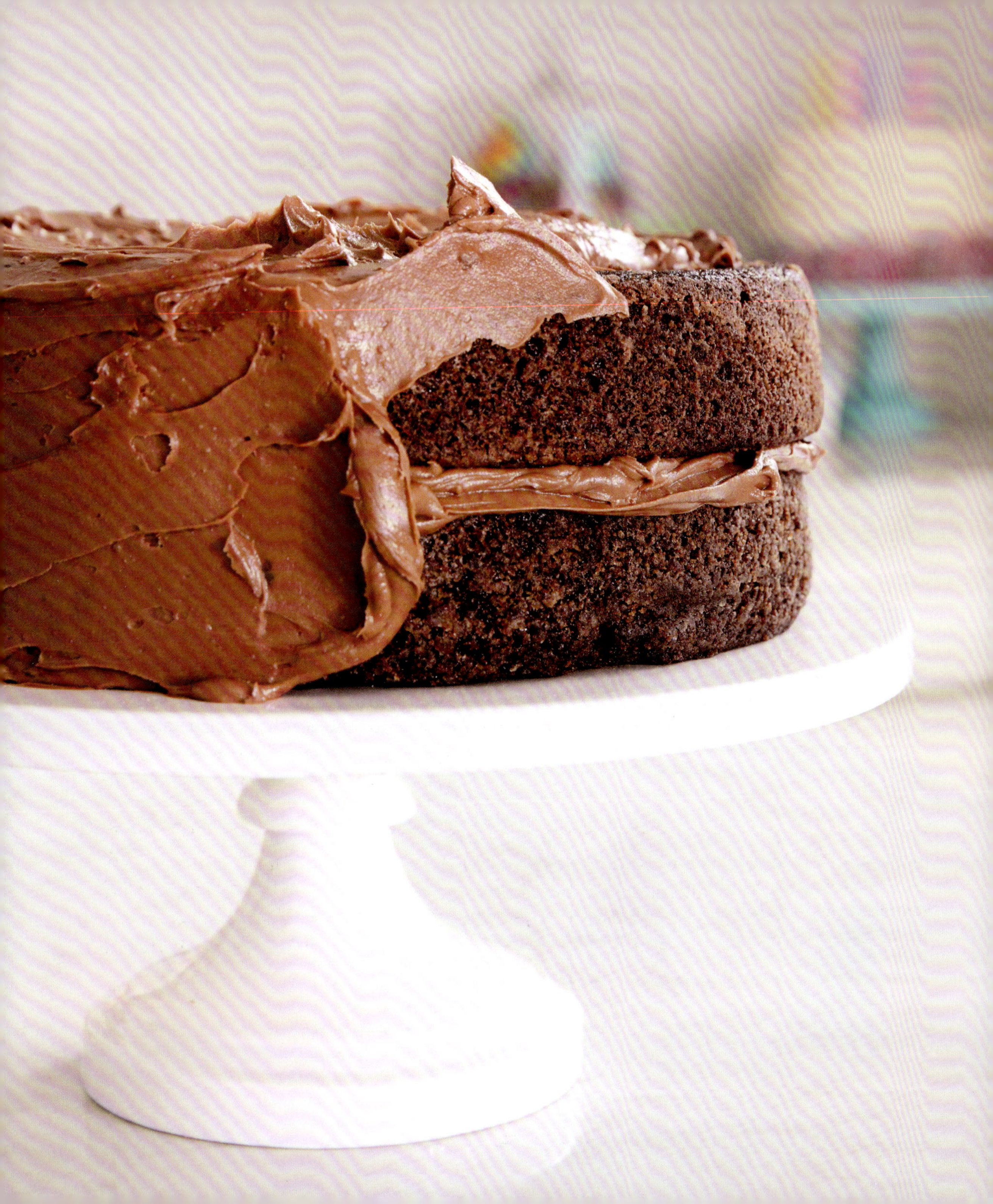

Dark Chocolate Frosting

MAKES ABOUT 4 CUPS

9 ounces bittersweet or semisweet chocolate, coarsely chopped

1½ cups unsalted butter, at cool room temperature

1 tablespoon whole milk

2 teaspoons vanilla extract

¼ teaspoon salt

2½ cups powdered sugar, sifted

In a small microwave-safe bowl, microwave the chocolate on high power, stopping and stirring every 30 seconds, until melted and smooth. Let cool until cool to the touch but still pourable.

In a medium bowl, using an electric mixer, beat the butter on medium-high speed until light and fluffy, about 2 minutes. On low speed, add the melted chocolate, milk, vanilla, and salt and beat until well blended. Stop the mixer and scrape down the bowl with a rubber spatula. On low speed, slowly add the sugar and beat until well blended and creamy. Increase the speed to high and beat until light and fluffy, about 1 minute.

Milk Chocolate Frosting

MAKES ABOUT 4 CUPS

6 ounces milk chocolate, coarsely chopped

3 ounces bittersweet chocolate, coarsely chopped

1½ cups unsalted butter, at cool room temperature

1 tablespoon whole milk

2 teaspoons vanilla extract

¼ teaspoon salt

2½ cups powdered sugar, sifted

In a small microwave-safe bowl, combine both chocolates and microwave on high power, stopping and stirring every 30 seconds, until melted and smooth. Let cool until cool to the touch but still pourable.

In a medium bowl, using an electric mixer, beat the butter on medium-high speed until light and fluffy, about 2 minutes. On low speed, add the melted chocolate, milk, vanilla, and salt and beat until well blended. Stop the mixer and scrape down the bowl with a rubber spatula. On low speed, slowly add the sugar and beat until well blended and creamy. Increase the speed to high and beat until light and fluffy, about 1 minute.

Chocolate Glaze

MAKES ABOUT 1½ CUPS

1 cup heavy cream

1 tablespoon light corn syrup

Pinch of salt

8 ounces semisweet chocolate, chopped

1 teaspoon vanilla extract

In a medium saucepan, combine the cream, corn syrup, and salt. Set the pan over medium heat and bring to a simmer (without boiling), stirring occasionally. Remove the pan from the heat, add the chocolate, and let stand for about 3 minutes.

Stir until the chocolate is completely melted and the mixture is smooth, then stir in the vanilla. Let cool to room temperature before using. The cooled glaze can be refrigerated in an airtight container for up to 3 days. To soften the glaze before using, heat gently in a heatproof bowl set over (not touching) barely simmering water in a saucepan.

Vanilla Glaze

MAKES ABOUT 1¾ CUPS

1½ cups powdered sugar

Pinch of salt

3 tablespoons unsalted butter, melted and cooled

2 tablespoons hot water, plus more if needed

1 teaspoon vanilla extract

Gel food coloring of choice (optional)

In a medium bowl, stir together the sugar and salt with a fork. In a small bowl, whisk together the butter, water, and vanilla. Add the butter mixture to the powdered sugar and whisk until smooth. Add a few drops of food coloring, if using, and stir to tint the glaze evenly. If the glaze is too thick, whisk in more hot water, 1 teaspoon at a time, until the desired consistency. Use right away.

Chocolate Sauce

MAKES ABOUT 1 CUP

6 ounces bittersweet chocolate, chopped

⅓ cup light corn syrup

⅓ cup whole milk

1 tablespoon unsalted butter

1 teaspoon vanilla extract

Fill a medium saucepan one-third full with water and heat until barely simmering over medium-low heat. Rest a heatproof bowl in the rim of the saucepan over (not touching) the water, add the chocolate and corn syrup, and heat, stirring often, until the chocolate has melted. Add the milk, butter, and vanilla and stir until blended. Remove from the heat.

Lemon Curd

MAKES ABOUT 1¼ CUPS

8 large egg yolks

1½ cups sugar

2 tablespoons finely grated lemon zest

¾ cup fresh lemon juice

¾ cup (1½ sticks) cold unsalted butter, cut into tablespoon-size pieces

In a medium saucepan, whisk together the egg yolks, sugar, and lemon zest and juice. Place over medium heat and cook, whisking often, until the mixture is thick enough to coat the back of a spoon, about 10 minutes. Add the butter and cook, stirring often, until melted, about 3 minutes. Reduce the heat to low and cook, whisking constantly, until the mixture starts to thicken, about 1 minute longer.

Remove from the heat and strain through a fine-mesh sieve into a heatproof bowl. Cover with plastic wrap, pressing it directly onto the surface of the curd (to prevent a "skin" from forming), and poke a few holes in the plastic to allow steam to escape. Let cool for several minutes, then refrigerate until well chilled, at least 2 hours or up to 3 days.

> ### Lime Curd
> Make the curd as directed, substituting ½ cup fresh lime juice and ¼ cup fresh lemon juice for the ¾ cup lemon juice.

Strawberry "Roses"

MAKES 6–8 LARGE "ROSES"

6–8 large strawberries, hulled and cored

Set a berry, stem end down, on a cutting board and, carefully using a paring knife, make a shallow vertical cut near the base of the berry. Using the edge of the knife, press down gently on the cut to fan the petal outward. Repeat, making as many petals around the base of the berry as desired. Cut and fan another row of petals slightly above the first row, layering them between the petals of the first row. Cut and fan a final row of petals near the tip of the berry. Make a shallow cut at the tip of the strawberry and, using the edge of the knife, gently nudge the top petals apart. Repeat with the remaining strawberries.

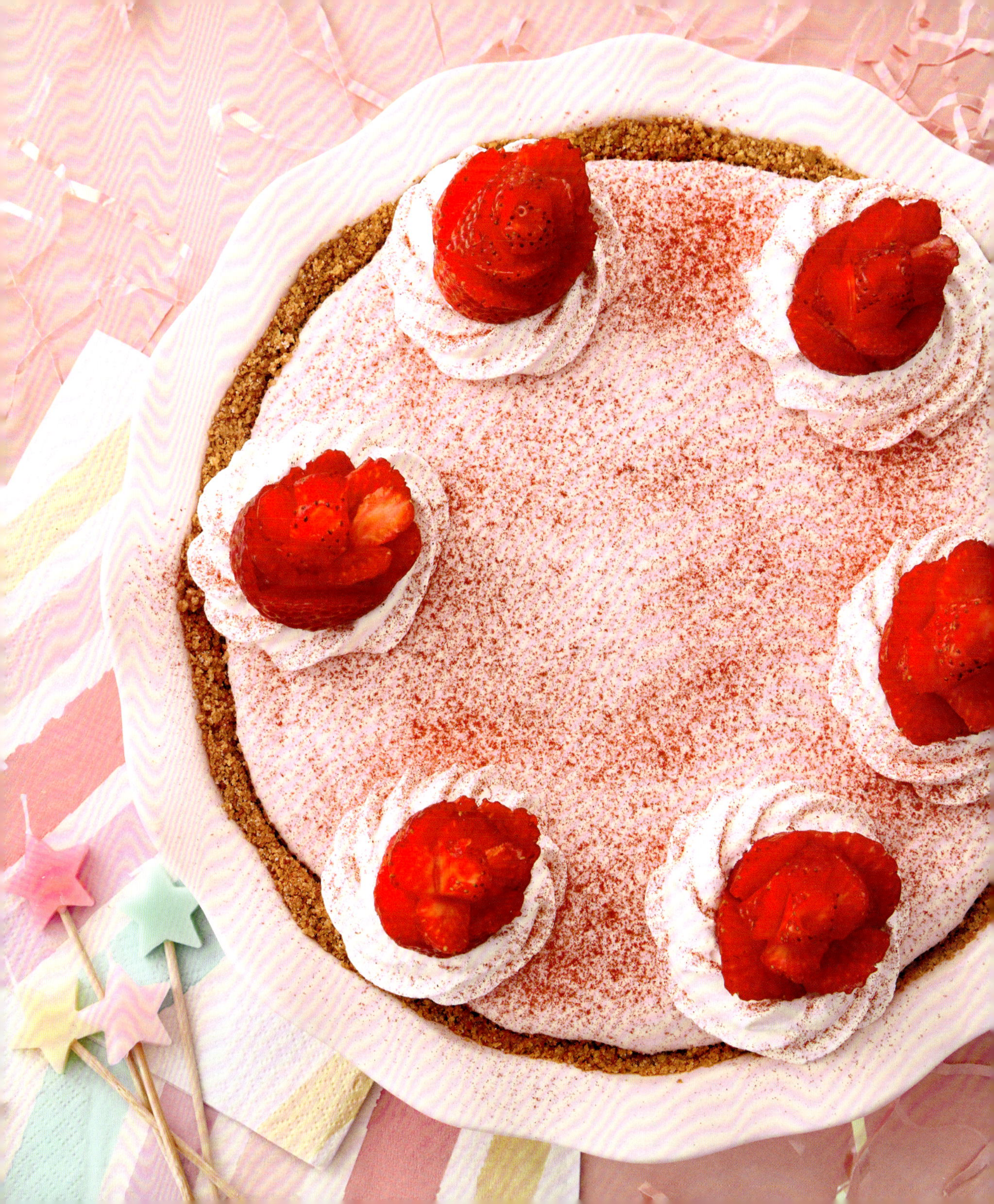

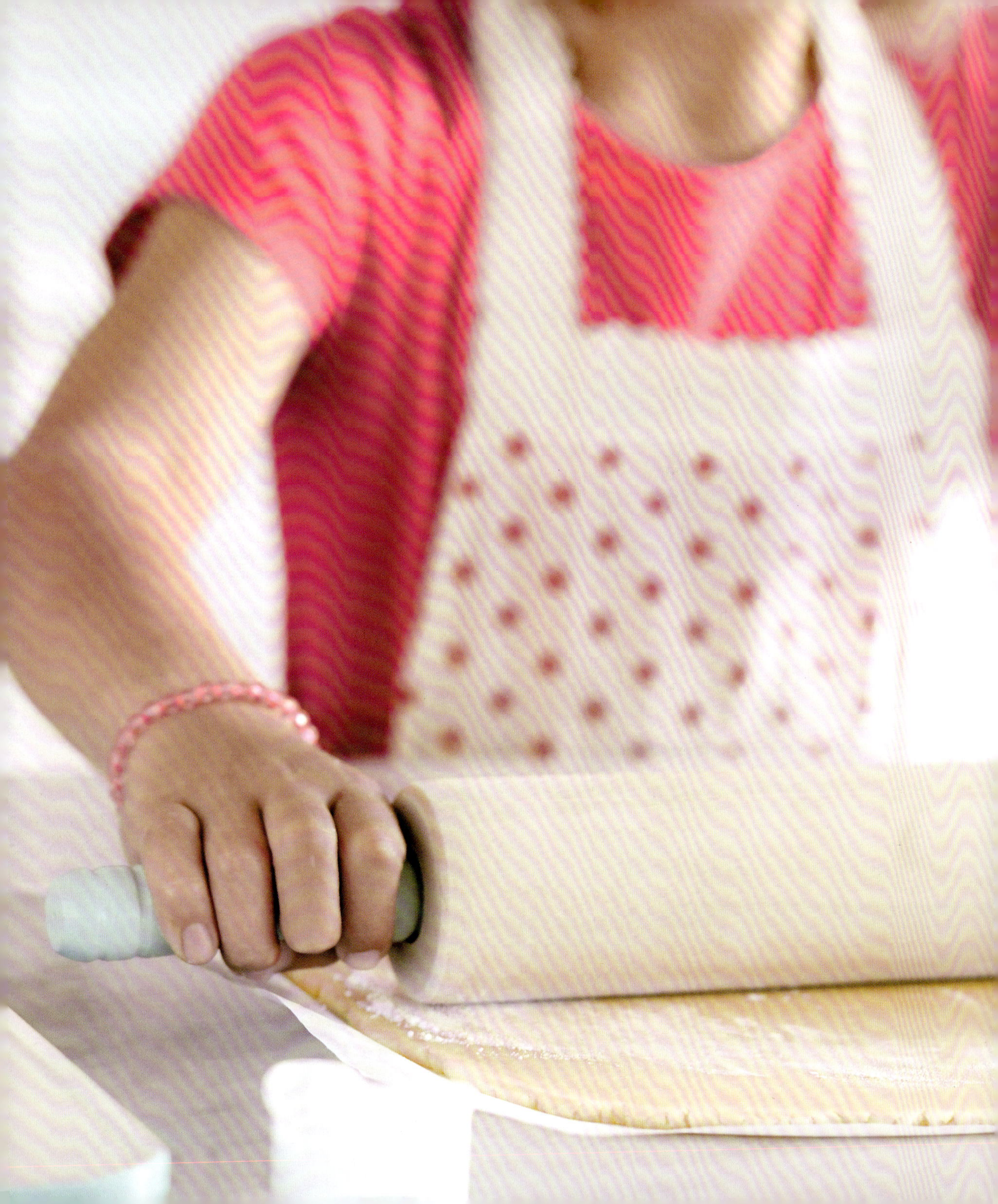

Flaky Pie Dough

MAKES ENOUGH FOR ONE 9-INCH SINGLE-CRUST PIE OR TWELVE 3-INCH TARTLETS

1½ cups all-purpose flour, plus more for the work surface

1 tablespoon sugar

¼ teaspoon salt

½ cup (1 stick) very cold unsalted butter, cut into cubes

6 tablespoons ice-cold water, plus more if needed

In a food processor, combine the flour, sugar, and salt and pulse a few times to mix. Scatter the butter over the flour mixture and pulse just until the butter is broken up into pieces the size of small peas. Evenly sprinkle the water over the flour-butter mixture, then process just until the mixture starts to come together in a shaggy dough, adding a little more water, 1 teaspoon at a time, if the dough crumbles when pinched between fingertips.

Turn the dough out onto a lightly floured work surface and press into a thick disk. Wrap tightly in plastic wrap and refrigerate for at least 30 minutes or up to 1 day before using. (The dough can also be frozen for up to 1 month; thaw in the refrigerator before using.)

Tart Dough

MAKES ENOUGH FOR ONE 9- OR 10-INCH TART OR TWELVE 3-INCH TARTLETS

1 large egg yolk

2 tablespoons ice-cold water

1 teaspoon vanilla extract

1¼ cups all-purpose flour, plus more for the work surface

¼ teaspoon salt

¼ cup sugar

½ cup cold unsalted butter, cut into cubes

In a small bowl, using a fork, stir together the egg yolk, water, and vanilla until blended. In a food processor, combine the flour, salt, and sugar and pulse a few times to mix. Scatter the butter over the flour mixture and pulse just until the butter is broken up into pieces the size of small peas. Pour the egg mixture evenly over the flour mixture, then process just until the mixture starts to come together in a shaggy dough.

Turn the dough out onto a lightly floured work surface and press into a thick disk. Wrap tightly in plastic wrap and refrigerate for at least 30 minutes or up to 1 day before using. (The dough can also be frozen for up to 1 month; thaw in the refrigerator before using.)

Index

A

Almonds
   Dulce de Leche Ice Cream Pie, 75
   Glazed Almond–Poppy Seed Mini Bundt Cakes, 28–30
   Vanilla Bean Cheesecake with Fresh Fruit, 48–49
Angel Food Strawberries and Cream Cake, 34–35
Apple Rose Tartlets, Spiced, with Caramel, 104–6

B

Baking sheets, rimmed, 11
Baking tips and hints
   adult help for recipes, 8
   all-star baking tips, 10
   baking tools, 11
   decorating guide, 13
Bananas
   Banana Chocolate Cream Pie, 110–11
   Chocolate Chip Chiffon Cake with Bananas and Caramel, 31–33
Berries
   Berries and Cream Roulade, 45–46
   Blackberry Cheesecake Cupcakes, 70
   Chocolate Raspberry Tartlets, 97–98
   Fruit and Cream Parfaits with Vanilla Shortbread, 123–24
   Raspberry-Swirled Pavlovas, 125–26
   Strawberries and Cream Puffs, 119
   Strawberry Mousse Pie, 94–96
   Strawberry "Roses," 146
   Tropical Fruit Cream Tart, 102–3
Blackberry Cheesecake Cupcakes, 70
Brownies
   Birthday Cake Brownies, 114
   Chocolate-Caramel Brownie Ice Cream Sundaes, 85
Butter, 10

C

Cakes
   Angel Food Strawberries and Cream Cake, 34–35
   Any-Kind-of-Ice-Cream Birthday Cake, 79–80
   Berries and Cream Roulade, 45–46
   Chocolate Chip Chiffon Cake with Bananas and Caramel, 31–33
   Chocolate-Mint Mini Ice Cream Cakes, 86
   Chocolate Mocha Dirt Sheet Cake, 36
   Chocolate Peanut Butter Bundt Cake, 26–27
   cooling, before frosting, 10
   decorating, 13
   Double Vanilla Ombré Cake, 20–21
   Eight-Layer Honey Pistachio Cake, 43–44
   Glazed Almond–Poppy Seed Mini Bundt Cakes, 28–30
   Lemon Meringue Layer Cake, 41–42
   Milk Chocolate Layer Cake, 19
   testing for doneness, 10
   Tres Leches Cake, 38–39
   Vanilla Bean Cheesecake with Fresh Fruit, 48–49
   Vanilla Confetti Birthday Cake, 22–25
Caramel
   Chocolate-Caramel Brownie Ice Cream Sundaes, 85
   Chocolate Chip Chiffon Cake with Bananas and Caramel, 31–33
   Millionaire's Shortbread, 128–29
   Spiced Apple Rose Tartlets with Caramel, 104–6
Cheesecake
   Blackberry Cheesecake Cupcakes, 70
   Vanilla Bean Cheesecake with Fresh Fruit, 48–49
Cherries
   Ice Cream Cone Cupcakes, 60
   Little Cherry Galettes, 99–101
Chocolate
   Any-Kind-of-Ice-Cream Birthday Cake, 79–80
   Banana Chocolate Cream Pie, 110–11
   Birthday Cake Brownies, 114
   Chocolate-Caramel Brownie Ice Cream Sundaes, 85
   Chocolate Chip Chiffon Cake with Bananas and Caramel, 31–33
   Chocolate Chip Cookie Dough Cupcakes, 57–58
   Chocolate Glaze, 144

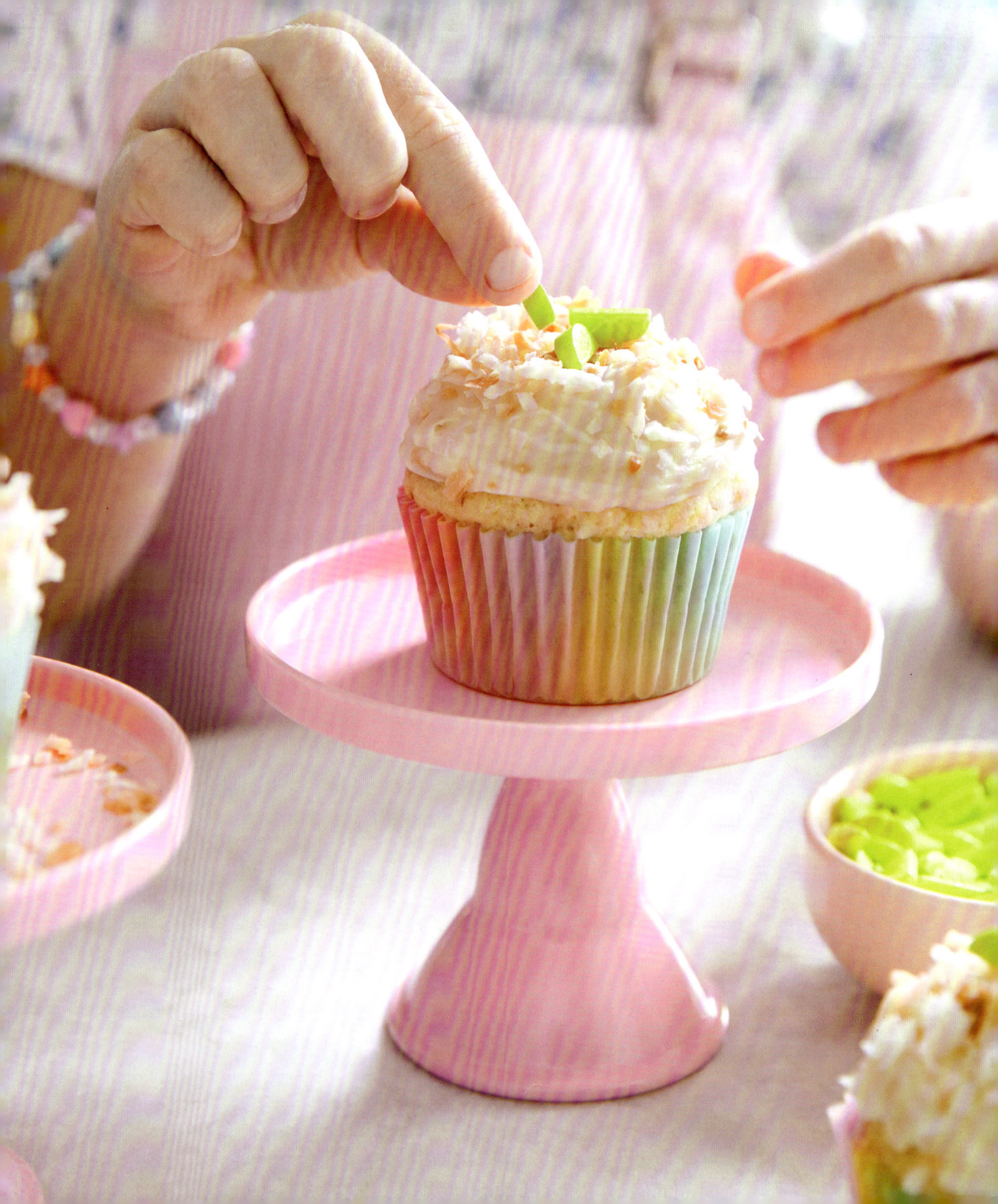

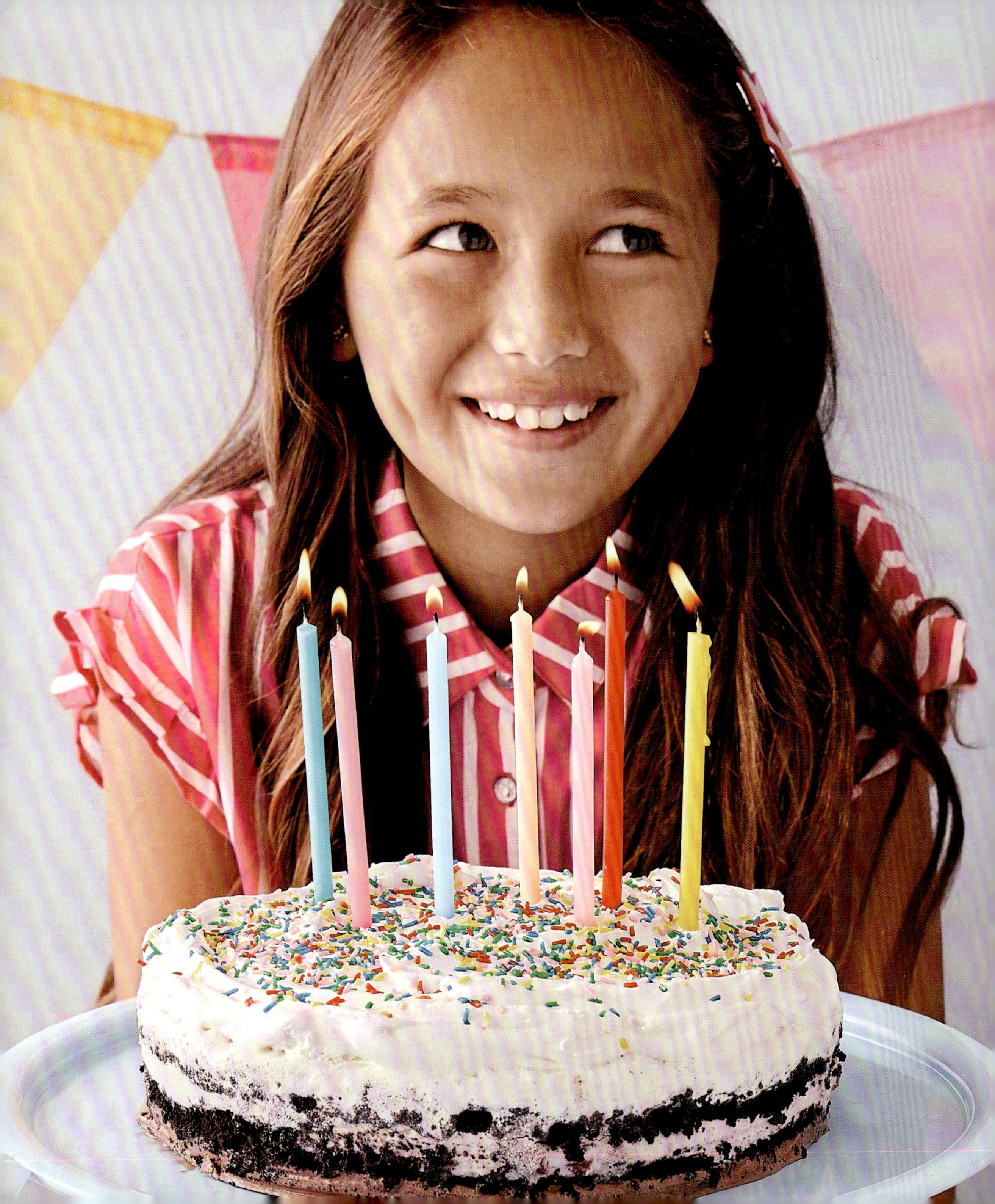

Chocolate-Glazed Doughnut Hole Cone Cake, 117–18
Chocolate-Mint Mini Ice Cream Cakes, 86
Chocolate Mocha Dirt Sheet Cake, 36
Chocolate Mousse Cups, 132
Chocolate Peanut Butter Bundt Cake, 26–27
Chocolate Raspberry Tartlets, 97–98
Chocolate Sauce, 145
Choco-Mallow Cupcakes, 63
Cinnamon-Sugar Churros with Chocolate Sauce, 120
Cookies and Cream Cupcakes, 59
Cookies and Cream Frosting, 135
Dark Chocolate Frosting, 143
Devil's Food Cupcakes, 64
Ice Cream Sandwiches, 76
Milk Chocolate Frosting, 143
Milk Chocolate Layer Cake, 19
Millionaire's Shortbread, 128–29
Mini Mint–Chocolate Chip Cupcakes, 65
Profiteroles with Ice Cream and Chocolate Sauce, 81–82
S'mores Tartlets, 93
Churros, Cinnamon-Sugar, with Chocolate Sauce, 120
Cinnamon-Sugar Churros with Chocolate Sauce, 120
Coconut-Lime Cupcakes, 66
Coffee. *See* Mocha
Cone Cake, Chocolate-Glazed Doughnut Hole, 117–18

Cookie Dough Frosting, 135
Cookies
   Ice Cream Sandwiches, 76
   Millionaire's Shortbread, 128–29
   Vanilla Shortbread, 123–24
Cookies and Cream Cupcakes, 59
Cookies and Cream Frosting, 135
Cream, Whipped, 140
Cream cheese
   Birthday Cake Brownies, 114
   Blackberry Cheesecake Cupcakes, 70
   Cream Cheese Frosting, 140
   Mini Red Velvet Cupcakes with Cream Cheese Frosting, 69
   Strawberry Mousse Pie, 94–96
   Vanilla Bean Cheesecake with Fresh Fruit, 48–49
Cupcake liners, 13
Cupcakes
   Blackberry Cheesecake Cupcakes, 70
   Chocolate Chip Cookie Dough Cupcakes, 57–58
   Choco-Mallow Cupcakes, 63
   Coconut-Lime Cupcakes, 66
   Cookies and Cream Cupcakes, 59
   cooling, before frosting, 10
   decorating, 13
   Devil's Food Cupcakes, 64
   Ice Cream Cone Cupcakes, 60
   Mini Mint–Chocolate Chip Cupcakes, 65
   Mini Red Velvet Cupcakes with Cream Cheese Frosting, 69

Rainbow Glitter Cupcakes, 53–54
testing for doneness, 10
Curd
   Lemon Curd, 145
   Lime Curd, 145

D

Decorating tips, 13
Devil's Food Cupcakes, 64
Dough
   Flaky Pie Dough, 149
   Tart Dough, 149
Doughnut Hole Cone Cake, Chocolate-Glazed, 117–18
Doughnuts, Unicorn Rainbow, 131
Dulce de Leche Ice Cream Pie, 75

E

Eggs, 10

F

Flaky Pie Dough, 149
Frostings
   Cookie Dough Frosting, 135
   Cookies and Cream Frosting, 135
   Cream Cheese Frosting, 140
   Dark Chocolate Frosting, 143
   Meringue Frosting, 139
   Milk Chocolate Frosting, 143
   Mint Frosting, 135
   Vanilla Frosting, 135

Frozen treats
    Any-Kind-of-Ice-Cream Birthday Cake, 79–80
    Chocolate-Caramel Brownie Ice Cream Sundaes, 85
    Chocolate-Mint Mini Ice Cream Cakes, 86
    Dreamy Orange and Vanilla Ice-Cream Pops, 87
    Dulce de Leche Ice Cream Pie, 75
    Ice Cream Sandwiches, 76
    Profiteroles with Ice Cream and Chocolate Sauce, 81–82
    Watermelon-Mint Ice Pops, 88
Fruit. *See also* Berries; *specific fruits*
    Fruit and Cream Parfaits with Vanilla Shortbread, 123–24
    Tropical Fruit Cream Tart, 102–3
    Vanilla Bean Cheesecake with Fresh Fruit, 48–49

G

Galettes, Little Cherry, 99–101
Glazes
    Chocolate Glaze, 144
    Vanilla Glaze, 144
Graham crackers
    Blackberry Cheesecake Cupcakes, 70
    S'mores Tartlets, 93
    Strawberry Mousse Pie, 94–96
    Vanilla Bean Cheesecake with Fresh Fruit, 48–49

H

Honey Pistachio Cake, Eight-Layer, 43–44

I

Ice cream
    Any-Kind-of-Ice-Cream Birthday Cake, 79–80
    Chocolate-Caramel Brownie Ice Cream Sundaes, 85
    Chocolate-Mint Mini Ice Cream Cakes, 86
    Dreamy Orange and Vanilla Ice-Cream Pops, 87
    Dulce de Leche Ice Cream Pie, 75
    Ice Cream Sandwiches, 76
    Profiteroles with Ice Cream and Chocolate Sauce, 81–82
Ice Cream Cone Cupcakes, 60
Ice cream scoop, 11
Ice Pops, Watermelon-Mint, 88

L

Lemon
    Glazed Almond–Poppy Seed Mini Bundt Cakes, 28–30
    Lemon Curd, 145
    Lemon Meringue Layer Cake, 41–42
Lime
    Coconut-Lime Cupcakes, 66
    Lime Curd, 145

M

Marshmallows and marshmallow creme
    Choco-Mallow Cupcakes, 63
    Rainbow Rice Crispy Pops, 133
    S'mores Tartlets, 93
Measuring cups and spoons, 11
Meringue Frosting, 139
Meringues. *See* Pavlovas
Millionaire's Shortbread, 128–29
Mint
    Chocolate-Mint Mini Ice Cream Cakes, 86
    Mini Mint–Chocolate Chip Cupcakes, 65
    Mint Frosting, 135
    Watermelon-Mint Ice Pops, 88
Mixers, 11
Mocha Chocolate Dirt Sheet Cake, 36
Mousse
    Chocolate Mousse Cups, 132
    Strawberry Mousse Pie, 94–96

N

Nuts. *See* Almonds; Pistachio

O

Offset spatulas, 11
Ombré Cake, Double Vanilla, 20–21
Orange and Vanilla Ice-Cream Pops, Dreamy, 87

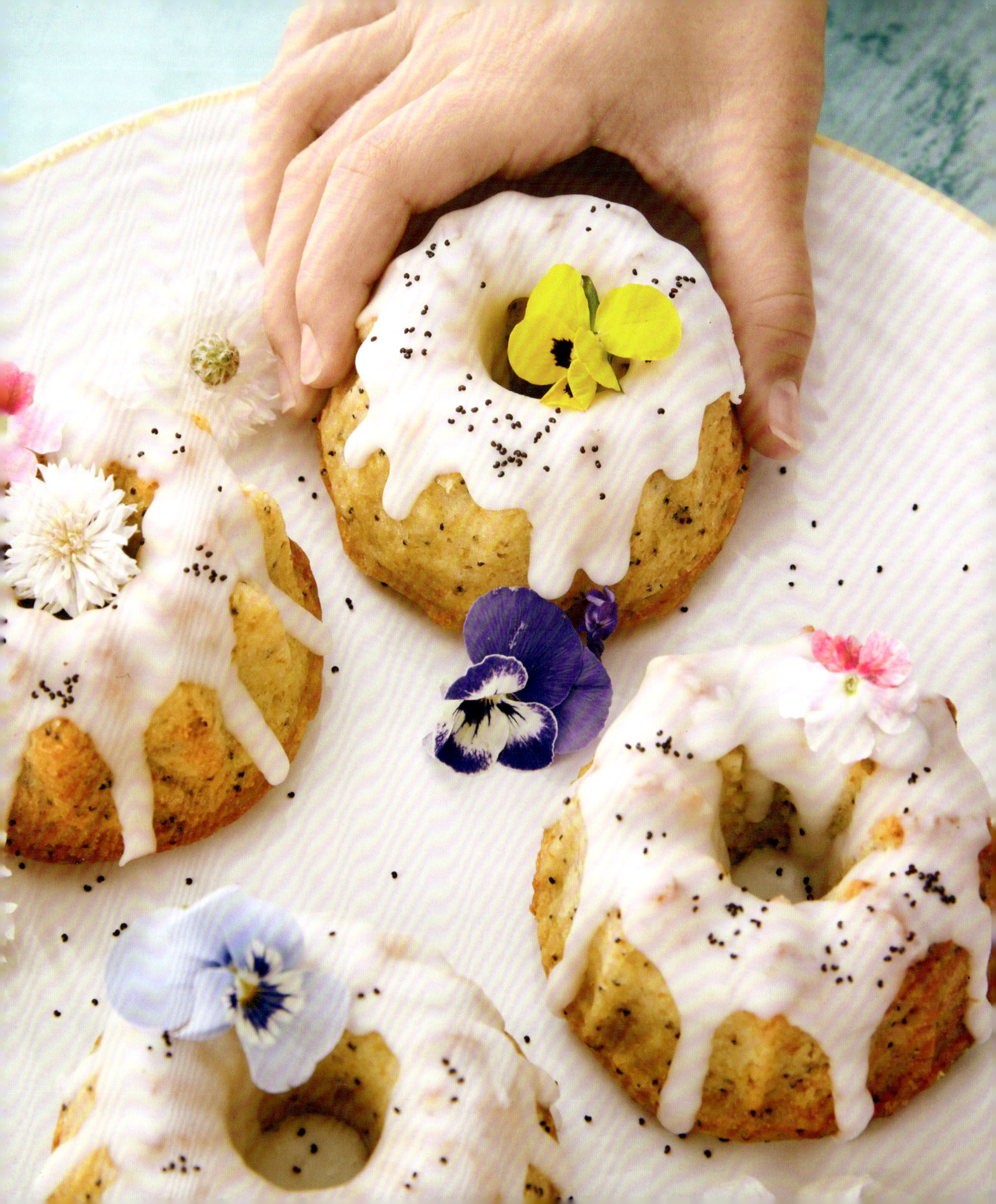

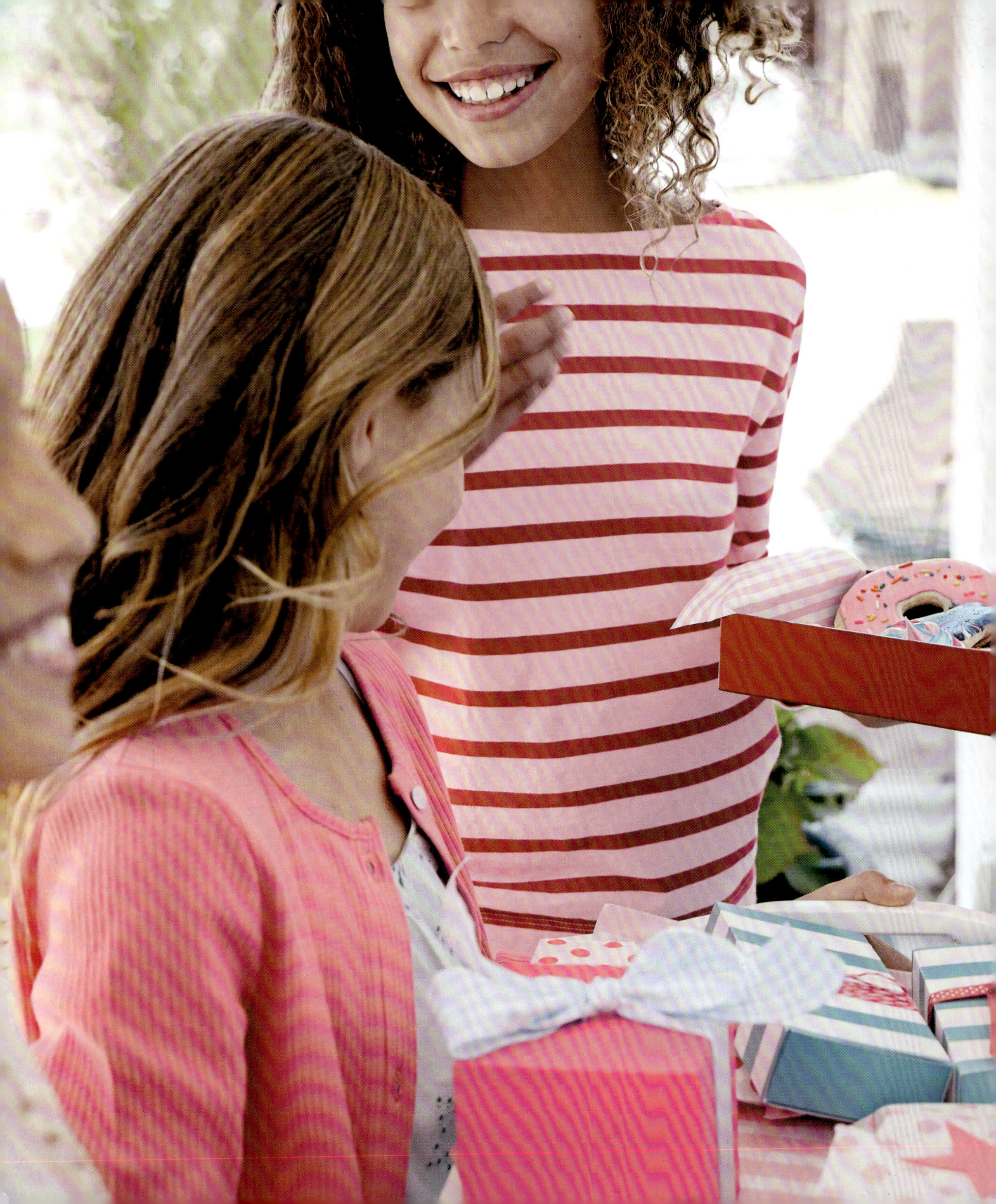

P

Parfaits, Fruit and Cream, with Vanilla Shortbread, 123–24
Pavlovas, Raspberry-Swirled, 125–26
Peach Slab Pie, 107–9
Peanut Butter Chocolate Bundt Cake, 26–27
Pie Dough, Flaky, 149
Pies and tarts
    Banana Chocolate Cream Pie, 110–11
    Chocolate Raspberry Tartlets, 97–98
    Dulce de Leche Ice Cream Pie, 75
    Little Cherry Galettes, 99–101
    Peach Slab Pie, 107–9
    S'mores Tartlets, 93
    Spiced Apple Rose Tartlets with Caramel, 104–6
    Strawberry Mousse Pie, 94–96
    Tropical Fruit Cream Tart, 102–3
Piping bag and pastry tips, 11, 13
Pistachio Honey Cake, Eight-Layer, 43–44
Poppy Seed–Almond Mini Bundt Cakes, Glazed, 28–30
Pops
    Dreamy Orange and Vanilla Ice-Cream Pops, 87
    Rainbow Rice Crispy Pops, 133
    Watermelon-Mint Ice Pops, 88
Profiteroles with Ice Cream and Chocolate Sauce, 81–82
Puffs
    Profiteroles with Ice Cream and Chocolate Sauce, 81–82
    Strawberries and Cream Puffs, 119

R

Rainbow Doughnuts, Unicorn, 131
Rainbow Glitter Cupcakes, 53–54
Raspberries
    Chocolate Raspberry Tartlets, 97–98
    Raspberry-Swirled Pavlovas, 125–26
Red Velvet Cupcakes, Mini, with Cream Cheese Frosting, 69
Rice Crispy Pops, Rainbow, 133
Rimmed baking sheets, 11
"Roses," Strawberry, 146
Rubber spatulas, 11

S

Sauce, Chocolate, 145
Shortbread
    Millionaire's Shortbread, 128–29
    Vanilla Shortbread, 123–24
S'mores Tartlets, 93
Spatulas, 11
Spoons, 11
Sprinkles, 13
    Any-Kind-of-Ice-Cream Birthday Cake, 79–80
    Birthday Cake Brownies, 114
    Chocolate-Glazed Doughnut Hole Cone Cake, 117–18
    Ice Cream Cone Cupcakes, 60
    Ice Cream Sandwiches, 76
    Rainbow Glitter Cupcakes, 53–54
    Rainbow Rice Crispy Pops, 133
    Unicorn Rainbow Doughnuts, 131
    Vanilla Confetti Birthday Cake, 22–25
Strawberries
    Angel Food Strawberries and Cream Cake, 34–35
    Berries and Cream Roulade, 45–46
    Strawberries and Cream Puffs, 119
    Strawberry Mousse Pie, 94–96
    Strawberry "Roses," 146
    Tropical Fruit Cream Tart, 102–3

T

Tart Dough, 149
Tarts. *See* Pies and tarts
Tres Leches Cake, 38–39
Tropical Fruit Cream Tart, 102–3

U

Unicorn Rainbow Doughnuts, 131

V

Vanilla
    Double Vanilla Ombré Cake, 20–21
    Dreamy Orange and Vanilla Ice-Cream Pops, 87
    Vanilla Bean Cheesecake with Fresh Fruit, 48–49
    Vanilla Confetti Birthday Cake, 22–25
    Vanilla Frosting, 135
    Vanilla Glaze, 144
    Vanilla Shortbread, 123–24

W

Watermelon-Mint Ice Pops, 88
Whipped Cream, 140
Whisks, 11

weldon**owen**

PO Box 3088 San Rafael, CA 94912
www.weldonowen.com

WELDON OWEN
CEO Raoul Goff
Publisher Roger Shaw

Associate Publisher Amy Marr
Publishing Director Katie Killebrew
Editorial Assistant Kayla Belser

VP of Creative Chrissy Kwasnik
Art Director Megan Sinead Bingham
Production Designer Jean Hwang
Senior Production Manager Joshua Smith
VP of Manufacturing Alix Nicholaeff

Photographer & Prop Stylist Nicole Hill Gerulat
Food Stylist Karen Evans
Photography Assistant Sam Wangberg

AMERICAN GIRL BIRTHDAY!
Conceived and produced by Weldon Owen International

A WELDON OWEN PRODUCTION
Copyright © 2024 Weldon Owen and American Girl
All rights reserved, including the right of reproduction in whole or in part in any form.
All American Girl trademarks are owned by and used under license from American Girl.

Printed and bound in China

First printed in 2024
10 9 8 7 6 5 4 3 2 1

Library of Congress Cataloging in Publication data is available

ISBN 13: 979-8-88674-133-9

ACKNOWLEDGMENTS
Weldon Owen wishes to thank the following people for their help in the production of this book:
Kim Laidlaw, Elizabeth Parson, and Sharon Silva.

A VERY SPECIAL THANK YOU TO
Our models: Ruby Gerulat, Harper Knudsen, Cambri Odei, and Leah Revelli

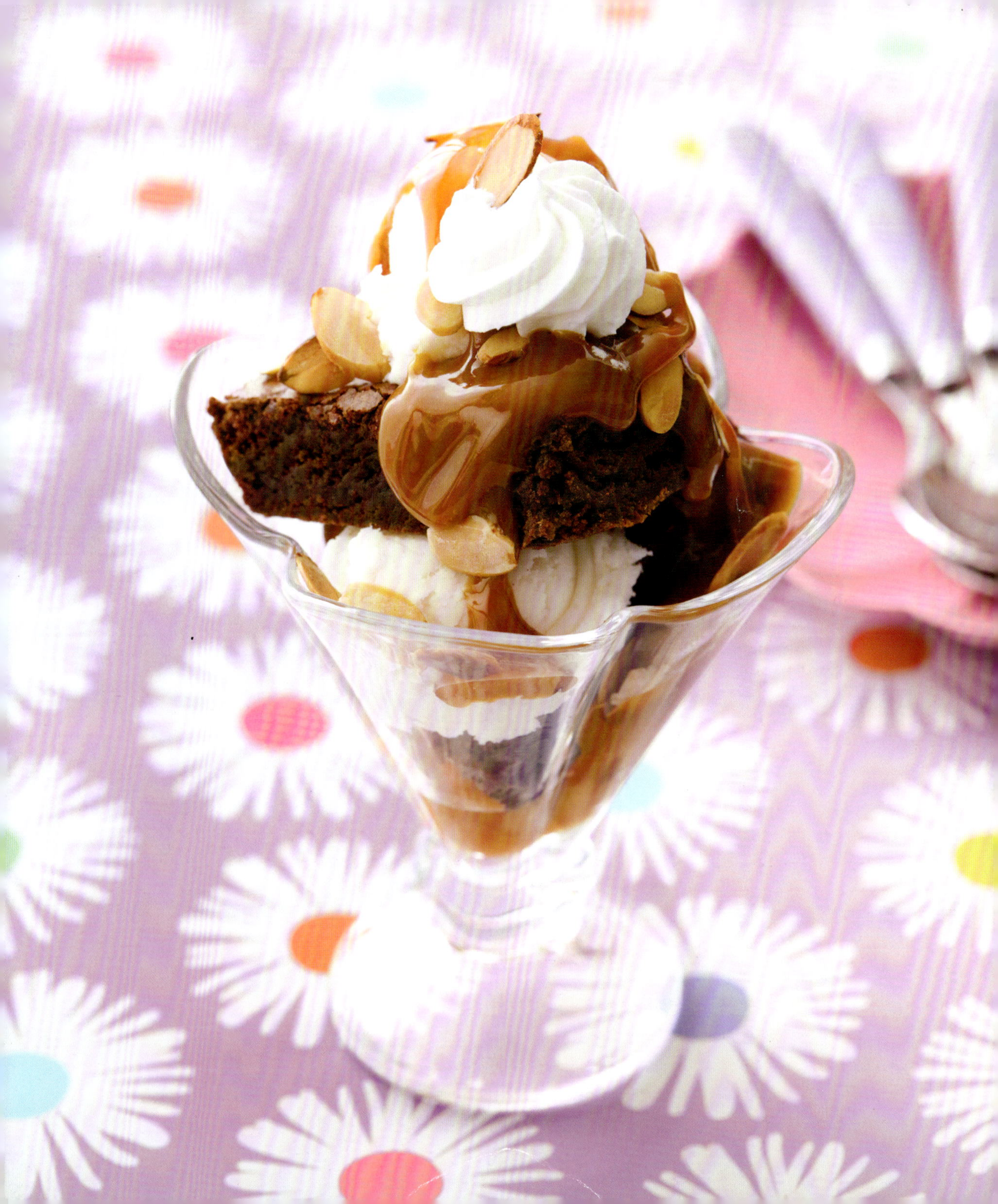

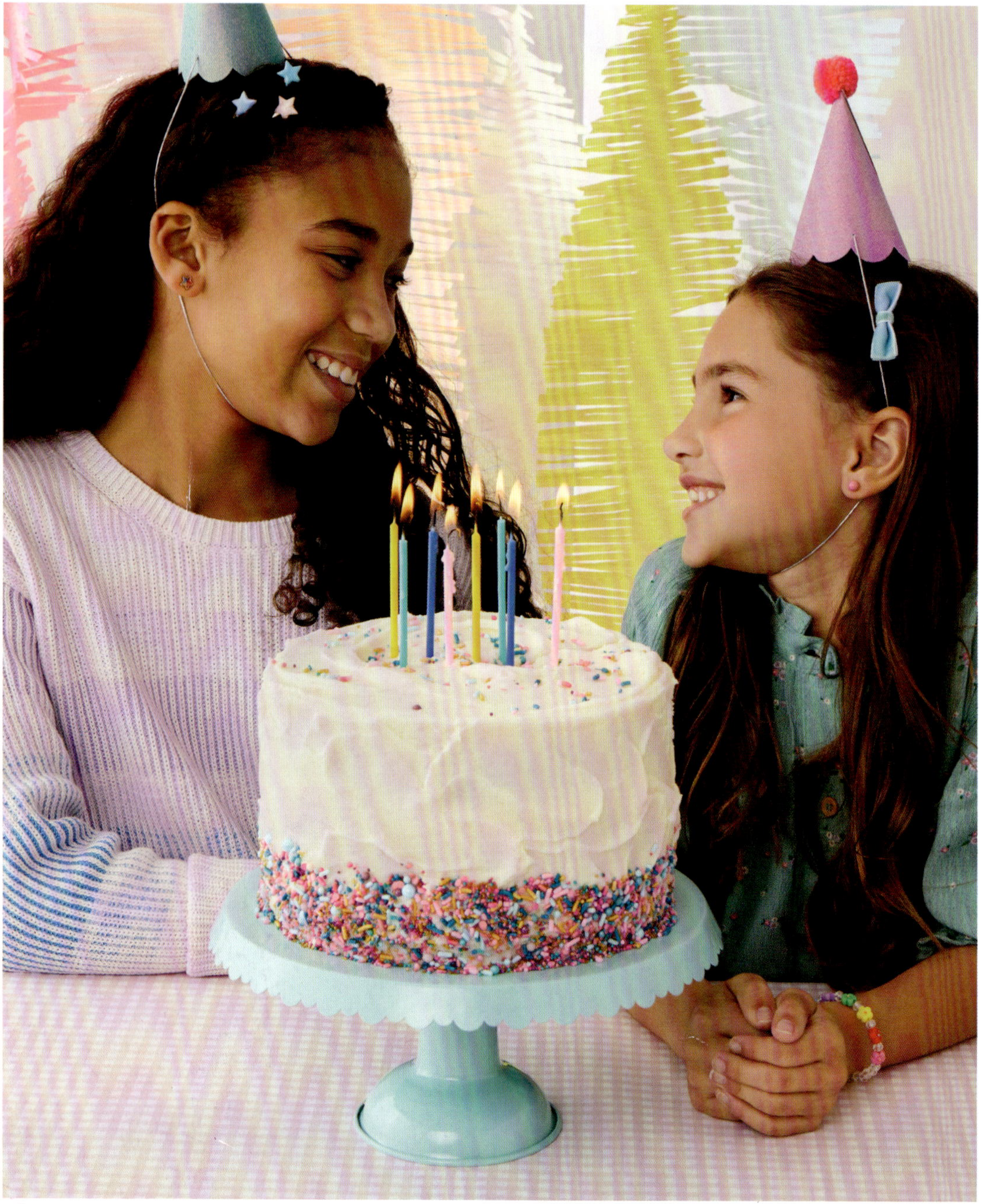

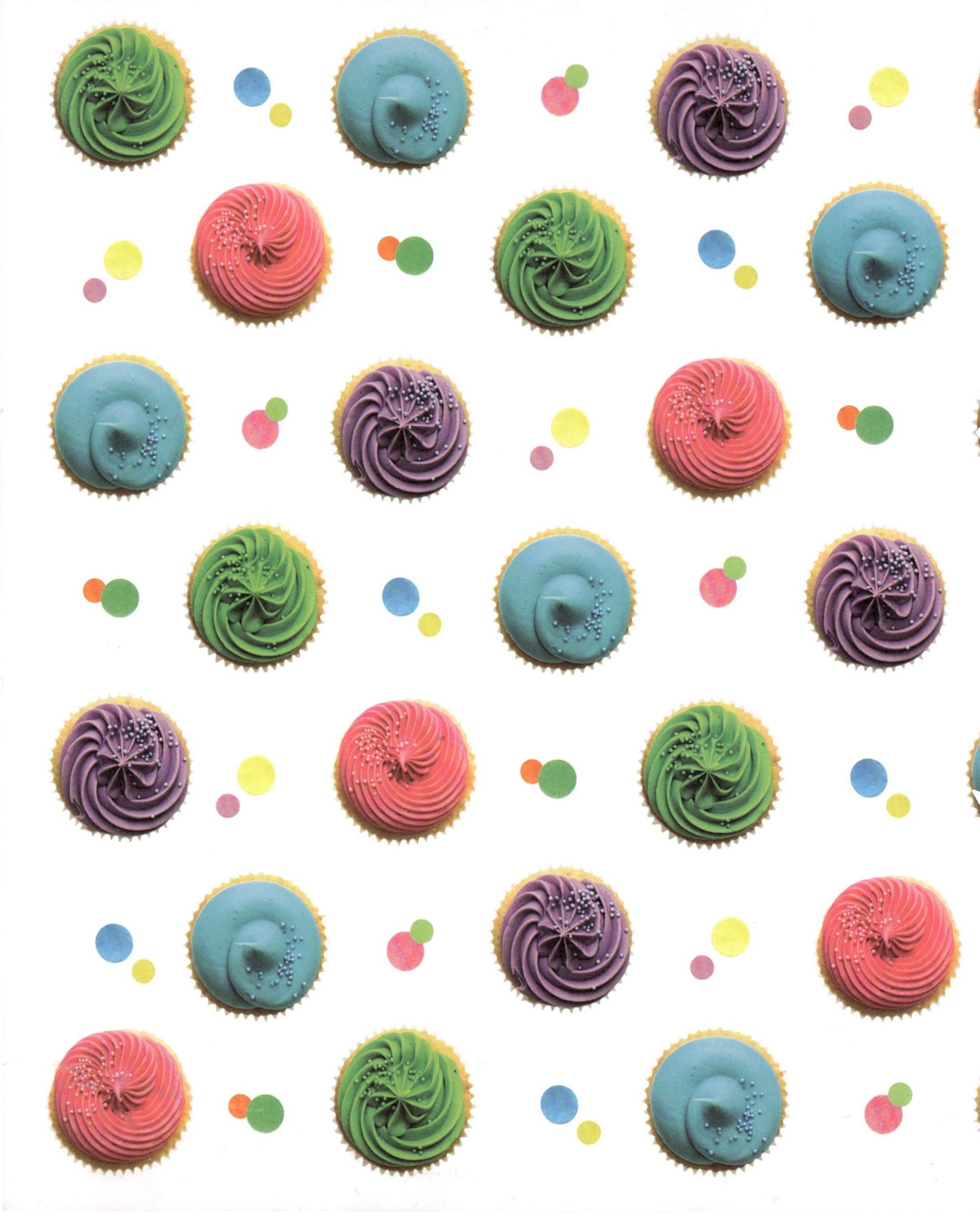